2 50

HORRIBLE SCIENCE

P9-DGZ-584

DISGUSTING DIGESTION

NICK ARNOLD

illustrated by
TONY DE SAULLES

SCHOLASTIC

Visit Nick Arnold at
www.nickarnold-website.com

Scholastic Children's Books,
Euston House, 24 Eversholt Street,
London, NW1 1DB, UK

A division of Scholastic Ltd
London ~ New York ~ Toronto ~ Sydney ~ Auckland
Mexico City ~ New Delhi ~ Hong Kong

First published in the UK by Scholastic Ltd, 1998
This edition published 2008

Text copyright © Nick Arnold, 1998
Illustrations © Tony De Saulles, 1998

ISBN 978 0439 94445 8

Printed in the UK by CPI Bookmarque, Croydon

10 9

The right of Nick Arnold and Tony De Saulles to be identified as the author and
illustrator of this work respectively has been asserted by them in accordance with
the Copyright, Designs and Patents Act, 1988.

CONTENTS

PSSSST, WANT THE INSIDE STORY ON DIGESTION, PAL?

Nick Arnold has been writing stories and books since he was a youngster, but never dreamt he'd find fame writing about Disgusting Digestion. His research involved battling with threadworms, bathing in stomach acid and eating pork pies and he enjoyed every minute of it.

When he's not delving into Horrible Science, he spends his spare time teaching adults in a college. His hobbies include eating pizza, riding his bike and thinking up corny jokes (though not all at the same time).

Tony De Saulles picked up his crayons when he was still in nappies and has been doodling ever since. He takes Horrible Science very seriously and even agreed to sample several school dinners for us. Fortunately, he has made a full recovery.

When he's not out with his sketchpad, Tony likes to write poetry and play squash, though he hasn't written any poetry about squash yet.

INTRODUCTION

Here's a disgusting science story…

It's ten minutes to the end of a particularly boring science lesson. The hands on the clock are crawling round like dozy snails. You're struggling to stay awake. It's so tedious.

So you try to think about something – anything to stop yourself from dropping off. Lunch, perhaps? Yes, that sounds like a good idea. OK – so it's only school lunch but breakfast was centuries ago. You're so hungry. Couldn't you just murder a scrumptious steaming pudding oozing with hot jam and custard?

But then your teacher asks a tricky question.

Dead silence.

No one answers. Just then your tum lets rip with a huge, hearty rumble. It sounds deafening – just like a massive rumble of thunder. The echoes bounce off the classroom walls. Everyone stares at you. What do you do?

a) Turn scarlet and mumble "Sorry".

b) Blame the smart, goody-goody kid next to you.

c) Jump up, and close all the classroom windows saying, "There must be a storm coming, wasn't that thunder?"

A scientist, of course, would know the scientific answer. Some scientists actually spend their lives delving into digestion. Digestion is when food is taken into your body to help you stay alive and grow. It sounds about as thrilling as last night's dirty dishes.

But it doesn't have to be.

Digestion is disgusting. Amazingly disgusting! And this disgustingly amazing process is going on inside your body right now. In this book there are some foul scientific secrets and disgusting discoveries served up with a hearty helping of belly-laughs. And afterwards you'll be able to Answer:your teacher's question like this…

* (Bor-bor-rig-mus) Posh medical term for a rumbling tummy. The stomach and gut walls squash the gas and liquids inside.

After all, there are plenty of laws in science but not one of them says it's got to be boring. So now there's only one question. Have you got the stomach for some really disgusting discoveries?

Better read on and find out…

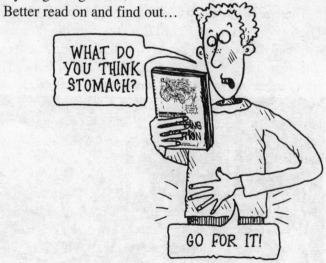

DISGUSTING DISCOVERIES

The young medical student turned white. His eyeballs bulged in his head and his mouth opened in a soundless scream. He wanted to yell but nothing came out. Not even a muffled gasp. He wanted to run. Run anywhere. But his legs wouldn't budge. He wanted to wake from his nightmare but this was no dream. It wasn't a scene from a horror film either. This was real life.

There really were sparrows flapping around the room. They were pecking at bits of dead body on the floor. And that really was a huge hungry rat skulking in the corner and gnawing greedily on a lump of human bone. This was a room in a hospital … and the year was 1821.

Don't panic! Hospitals aren't like this any more. But when 18-year-old medical student Hector Berlioz (1803–1869) visited a dissecting room in Paris this is what he really saw. (A dissecting room was where dead bodies were cut up so that their different parts could be studied.) This is just one example of the disgusting conditions endured by doctors and scientists in the past as they probed the secrets of digestion.

DISGUSTING DIGESTION DATES

The ancient Egyptians were into dissecting 5,000 years ago. In fact, every time they made a mummy they got their hands on the human guts. They always removed the intestines, or guts, and other vital organs and put them into jars because they would rot easily and spoil the preserved mummy. They kept all the body bits in jars for the mummy to use in the afterlife.

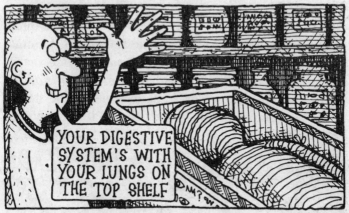

YOUR DIGESTIVE SYSTEM'S WITH YOUR LUNGS ON THE TOP SHELF

But the Egyptians weren't interested in the structure of the guts or how they worked. One of the first people to be genuinely interested in the guts was a foul-tempered Roman doctor.

Hall of fame: Claudius Galen (AD129–201)
Nationality: Roman
Galen said:

Hope your mum isn't like that. Sadly Galen inherited his mum's temper and nothing much from his dad.

Young Galen was disgustingly clever. He wrote three books before he was 13 and another 500 after that. Some of them had intriguing titles like *Bones for Beginners*, *On the Black Bile*, and *On the Usefulness of Parts of the Body*. One day Galen kept 12 scribes busy as he strode up and down dictating the words for 12 different books at the same time.

Galen reckoned he had the last word on medicine. He once said:

Whoever seeks fame needs only become familiar with all that I have achieved.

Modest, eh? The problem was Galen wasn't always right. In fact he was often WRONG. For example, he reckoned blood was made in the guts and went to the liver where it turned blue.

WRONG. Blood is made in the bone marrow and spleen. Just goes to show you can't believe everything you read in books. Mind you, Galen wasn't the only one – in his day many people thought that men had more teeth than women. WRONG – it's incredible they never bothered to count them!

DO YOU MEAN I'M NOT NORMAL?

Galen made silly mistakes because he got his ideas from cutting up dead animals rather than humans. But no doctors dared to argue with him. They were scared of Galen's famously foul temper. (Once Galen had even dared to shout insults at an opponent in the sacred

Temple of Peace.) And they were even more scared he might ask his pal the Roman Emperor to dispose of them in a disgusting fashion.

For about 1,500 years doctors believed Galen's theories. They could have cut up a few bodies to check for themselves. But few did. Governments often banned dissection and where it *was* allowed doctors felt they were too grand for all the messy, gory cutting up stuff and left that to their humble assistants. Then a doctor came along who was…

A CUT ABOVE THE REST

Whilst he studied in the Belgian town, Andreas Versalius (1514–1564) had a horrible habit. He stole dead bodies. And he wasn't particular either – anybody's body would do. Young, old, men or women – it didn't matter as long as the corpse wasn't too rotten. While he worked in the Belgian town of Louvain he used some disgustingly dodgy tricks to gain his revolting ends. He would:

• dig up bodies in cemeteries.

• steal the bodies of criminals left on public display.

• attend executions and sneak the body away at the end of the proceedings.

Then he would hide the bodies in his room. And late into the night by the flickering flame of a candle, he probed their grisly innards. Andreas Versalius wasn't crazy. He was a scientist and he was determined to go to any lengths to solve the mysteries of how the body worked. The appalling methods he used were the only way to get any answers. Dissection was banned, remember.

Things became easier in 1536 when Versalius became Professor of Anatomy in Padua, Italy. Here, the authorities were sympathetic to dissection. They even fixed execution dates so that the criminal's body would be nice and fresh for anatomy classes.

You'll be pleased to know doctors no longer need to steal bodies to practise dissection. Some people actually agree to allow their bodies to be dissected after death to help train medical students.

Bet you never knew!
Here's how to play Andreas Versalius's favourite game.
1 Allow yourself to be blindfolded.
2 Ask your friends to hand you a selection of human bones.
3 Identify them by their shape and the way they feel.
4 You win if you get them all right.

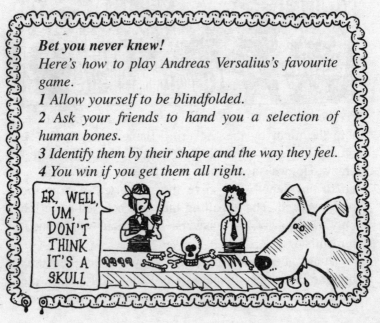

ROTTEN READING

Versalius discovered more about the inside of the human body than anyone before him. He was the first person to describe the structure of the human guts accurately. In 1543 he published his discoveries in a book *The Fabric of the Human Body*. It was packed with tasteful pictures of bits of bodies and skeletons with lovely scenery to make the revolting subject matter nicer to look at. The book was a bestseller.

SKELETON RECLINING IN A FIELD OF DAFFODILS – NICE!

But Versalius came to a disgusting end. According to one story he was cutting up a nobleman's body when it twitched. The "corpse" was still alive! Versalius decided to make himself scarce and embarked on a long sea voyage. But poor old Versalius was shipwrecked and starved to death on a lonely island. And what's more he had no body to keep him company!

IF ONLY I HAD MY TOOLBOX I COULD GET THE SEAGULL I ATE FOR BREAKFAST OUT OF MY STOMACH AND EAT IT AGAIN FOR DINNER

Could you have made these disgusting discoveries? Here's your chance to probe those gruesome innards and their grisly secrets. Delicate readers may find this next chapter not quite to their taste. It's a little bit sick.

DISGUSTING DIGESTIVE BITS'N'PIECES

Would you want to inspect the guts in grisly close-up detail? It's a horrible job but sometimes it's vital to check on problems. The scientist in this chapter has a real problem. He was absent-mindedly sucking his pen when he swallowed the top. It got stuck somewhere in his guts.

As luck would have it he'd just invented an incredible shrinking machine.

So all he needed was a volunteer to shrink down to 2.5 cm high and venture into his guts in search of the missing top. Any takers? Unfortunately, every doctor the scientist asked seemed to have an excuse. So he hired hard-bitten Private Eye, M I Gutzache for this unpleasant job.

First Gutzache had to change into special protective clothing so he wouldn't be digested during his hazardous mission.

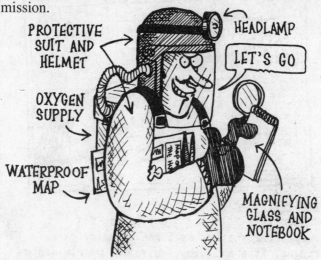

Here's Gutzache's report. Go on take a look, you know you want to – it's fascinating.

It seemed a cinch. Just a quick surveillance operation. "No problem," I said. So I took the job. That was my first big mistake. I may be a small-time private eye but under the shrinking ray I started to feel even smaller. But the worst was yet to come. I was going to be swallowed by a scientist!

Tough teeth

The teeth looked tough. There were several types. Some geared for biting, and some for chewing, gnawing or nibbling. They all looked mighty mean to me. Teeth are as hard as they come – d'you know you need a diamond to cut into them?

ARE YOU SURE YOU BRUSHED THEM THIS MORNING, DOC?

Tasteful tongue

Suddenly, I felt the floor heave. Not surprising really, as I was standing on a tongue. It's a living, quivering muscle and a real smart mover. While the scientist guy was talking, his tongue tossed a lump of carrot into a huge puddle of spit, and another piece came flying in between his teeth. It's awesome

what that muscle can do! But if I didn't act
fast I figured I'd be next for a spit dunking.
I cast around for an exit.

Salivary (sal-i-very) glands

But I was too late, all of a sudden I felt
wet and hot. Looking down I saw I was up to
my knees in saliva (that's spit to you). It
looked like trouble - but trouble is my
business. I knew there were six hidden glands
pumping this stuff out. I was going to have
to swim for it. I dived down the gullet. It
seemed the safest place to be. But I was wrong.

The scientist writes…

I was trying hard not to bite Detective Gutzache.
It was actually quite lucky that he fell into my saliva –
it helped me to swallow him. Spit may seem disgusting
stuff, but it's full of proteins called enzymes.

1. A food molecule (molecule = group of atoms) slots
into an enzyme molecule.

2. A chemical reaction takes place in which the food
molecule gets broken up into smaller molecules that can
pass through my gut walls. (This happens all the time
in my small intestine!)

Then disaster struck. Gutzache got stuck in my gullet, or oesophagus (a-sof-fer-gus), to use the technical term. What would happen to him now?

Oesophagus

Just my luck to get wedged in his throat! The scientist guy started coughing and spluttering. My body shook as he gulped. Then I felt all this water flooding over me – I was on the move! Now, I often find myself in tight spots and I can tell you this next one was seriously tight. The sides of his gullet squeezed together forcing me down. Then I hit some half-chewed food. The gullet walls squeezed the food into a ball. I knew that I could be squashed too. I wanted out. But it was too late.

STOP SWALLOWING DOC!

The scientist adds…

My oesophagus walls squeezed together behind Mr Gutzache and pushed him down. This is called peristalsis (perry-stal-sis). It's Greek for "push around". It was lucky he didn't fall down my windpipe. That would have started me choking until I'd coughed him back into my mouth.

Stomach

I hit the stomach with a splash. It was more of a bellyflop than a dive. I found myself swimming in a lake of mush. It looked and smelled like sick. It was sick! I felt sick too. I was churned around as the stomach walls squeezed in and out. I felt like a sock in a washing machine. I figured the juice was acid because I could see it dissolving the food. I was real glad of my protective suit!

CURRY AND RICE PUDDING, YUCK!

The scientist writes…

My stomach lining makes up to 2 litres of acid juice every day to dissolve the food I eat. And there are enzymes at work too.

Small intestine

After a few hours I managed to squeeze through the exit below the stomach. I found myself in a long tube that looked like a subway. I switched on my headlamp and peered at my waterproof map. My route was clear. I should head down the duodenum (dew-o-dee-num), jejunum (gee-june-num) and ileum (ill-ee-um). Whatever they were.

21

The map said "small intestine" – but it seemed endless. I knew I had to keep moving. The gut walls were closing behind me and I wasn't hanging around to get squashed again. So I walked. My feet squashed on the soft rubbery ground. Just then I saw something large and blue trapped in a fold in the wall. Success! It was the missing pen top. I gingerly pulled it out and tucked it under my arm. Now all I had to do was to get out without getting digested on the way.

A squirt

Suddenly I was splattered with digestive juices. I felt like an automobile in a car-wash, except I wasn't getting any cleaner. I was covered in brownish slimy bile from the liver and pale juice from the pancreas, I didn't stop to admire the view. I made tracks for the large intestine.

The scientist writes…

It's me again. I just wanted to explain that my bile breaks up the remains of greasy, fatty foods. It comes from my gall bladder, which is a little bag under the liver. My pancreas is about 18cm long and it's draped under my stomach. Besides enzymes, it makes vital chemicals that control the amount of sugar in my blood.

Appendix

In the large intestine I saw a weird sight. A little tube, about 5cm long, leading to a dead end. In the end I figured it out. It was the appendix. It wasn't doing much — just hanging out, I guess.

The scientist writes...

Gutzache's got it right for once! My appendix spends its life doing nothing and I'm not even sure why it's there. My large intestine is definitely there for a reason though, it sucks up any spare water and minerals from my food.

The rectum

I was dead beat. So I sat down. Big mistake. I sank into something soft and brown and it didn't smell too good. I was in the rectum. It was the final stretch of the large intestine. And there was only one way out. I could see the toilet bowl. It seemed a long way down but there was nowhere else to go. I shoved the pen top out and it splashed into the water far below. *My turn next*, I thought.

The scientist writes…

The large intestine is where waste food is stored. Most of the spare water is sucked out of the waste and through the sides of the gut. Er . . . 'scuse me a minute. Got to dash . . .

Splash-down
It was time to check out. I never liked parachute jumps. After I crawled out of the water I quit the job. The scientist wanted me to check out his liver but I'd had enough. I needed a vacation. Fighting violent crime seemed easy after this.

DISGUSTING EXPRESSIONS

Answer: Hope not. This is the medical word for a lump of poo. The main reason why doctors say "stool" is that they'd feel silly saying "poo" all day. So when you visit the doctor make sure that you don't ask for a stool to sit on. By the way the other medical word for poo is faeces (fee-sees).

Bet you never knew!

1 Some people have worms in their guts. It's true! Roundworms, pin worms and flukes can all live in the guts and feast on half-digested food. They generally get there in infected food. And once in, they lay eggs that pass out of the body with the faeces ready to infect someone else. But don't panic! Nowadays these nasty little suckers can be beaten using drugs.

2 The gut also contains microbiological* bacteria or as you might know them – germs. Up to 500 types of bacteria happily splash around in your guts where they make nasty smells. And they make up over 1 kg of your total weight! But most of them are harmless and some even make useful K and B vitamins to keep us healthy (see pages 77–80 for more details).

*Microbiological means the study of tiny life. Go on, say it. It's a brilliant word to chuck into a Friday afternoon science lesson. It means you need a microscope to see these bacteria because they're so small. You could actually find hundreds on the pointy end of a pin.

25

MORE BITS 'N' PIECES

In his hurry to get away, Gutzache missed out a few important digestive bits and pieces. It's time to take a closer look at…

The life-saving liver

Tiny bits of digested food molecules in the blood go to the liver to make vital substances your body needs. The liver also does hundreds of other vital jobs such as making bile (see page 22).

The vagus (vay-gus) nerve

The vagus nerve is like a long telephone wire that "vaguely" snakes round the guts carrying messages to and from the brain. These include orders to squeeze the gut wall and move the food ball on to its next destination.

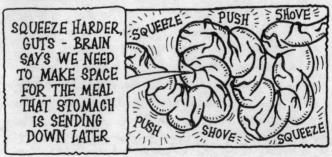

Crucial kidneys

These are the body's filters. As blood passes through them they clear out all the spare water and waste products and send them down for storage in the bladder.

Bursting bladder

This is an incredibly wrinkled sack. It looks like a prune after a really long bath, but as it fills up, it gets bigger and it looks more like a balloon. The speed this happens depends on how much a person has had to drink. Most people need to pee about four to six times a day.

How can you tell when someone's bladder is full? Easy. They start twitching, writhing and dancing around looking for the nearest loo. If you were feeling heartless you could...

a) Join in the dancing.

THAT'S REALLY GROOVY. LET'S ALL DANCE, WEEEE!

b) Tell them not to worry – the bladder can store up to 400 ml of pee (or urine, to use the posh word for it) fairly easily.

In fact, the bladder is so strong that in an adult it can swell to 10 cm across without going pop.

DISGUSTINGLY ODD BITS'N' PIECES QUIZ

Now you've checked out the main digestive bits, you've just got time to check out the obscure nooks and crannies. Doctors were probably having a laugh when they dreamt up some of the weird names for certain body bits. Can you guess which bits are inside you and which are made up?

1 Deaver's Windows
2 Islets of Langerhans
3 Crypt of Lieberkühn
4 The Pustule of Volvo
5 Flint's Arcade
6 Ferrein's Pyramid
7 Fibres of Mummery
8 Verheyen's Stars

IS THIS MY PUSTULE OF VOLVO, SIR?

NO, THAT'S YOUR NOSE, SMITH

CLASS 4

Answers: 1 TRUE. These are spaces in the flesh that hold the guts securely in position. The spaces are named after their discoverer, American scientist John Blair Deaver. **2 TRUE.** These are areas in the pancreas which make a hormone called insulin that controls the speed your body stores energy in the form of fats or sugars. They're named after eagle-eyed German doctor Paul Langerhans who spotted them in 1869. **3 TRUE.** And what's more they aren't crypts where dead bodies are buried. They're tiny pits in the small intestine that produce digestive juices. But you'd be a dead body without them because they're vital to digest your food. **4 FALSE.** The Volvo is a Swedish car. **5 TRUE.** These are arch-shaped blood vessels in the kidneys and nothing to do with amusement arcades. They're named after their discoverer, American professor Austin Flint. **6 TRUE.** An area of the kidney above Flint's arcade. These pyramid-shaped bits were named after a French professor of surgery called Antoine Ferrein, who wrote about them in 1746. They're nothing to do with the pyramids in Egypt and you won't find a mummy skulking inside one. **7 TRUE.** These are stringy bits inside the teeth. They're nothing to do with mummies or pyramids either. **8 TRUE.** These are star-shaped veins on the kidney named after Philipe Verheyen who described them in 1699. Verheyen was planning to be a priest but he had an accident and doctors had to chop his leg off. He was so fascinated by this horrible ordeal that he gave up the priesthood. He decided to study medicine instead and became a professor.

Congratulations! You've finished the chapter. Feeling peckish? Desperate enough to eat a school dinner? Better scoff some now before you read about the vile food in the next chapter. It really takes the cake ... or is it the biscuit?

FOUL FOOD FACTS

This chapter is about food. It's about what we eat and how much we eat. But don't expect a mouth-watering feast. This is Horrible Science, remember, so you'll be reading about really foul foods. Got a brown paper bag handy? Good – you might need it!

THAT'S AMAZING! WE HAD SWEETCORN FOR DINNER, TOO!

ENORMOUS EATERS

In your lifetime you'll guzzle about 30 tonnes of food – that's the weight of six elephants or 20 rhinos. In one year the average greedy grown-up can munch their way through 34 kg of potatoes, 11.8 kg of sugar, 500 apples, 150 loaves of bread and 200 eggs, and still have room for pudding.

STOP MOANING BERNARD, WE ONLY GO SHOPPING ONCE A YEAR.

SUPERM

If you only ate boring pieces of bread and butter all the time you'd still get through about 250,000 slices in a lifetime. But some people eat a lot more than that.

All-time glutton Edward "Bozo" Miller of Oakland, California used to guzzle 11 times more food than anyone else. In 1963 he scoffed 28 chickens in a single stomach-splitting feast and became a legend in his own lunchtime. Now you might think that's a lot, but compared with some animals it's just a tiny snack.

• An elephant can knock back up to half a tonne of leaves and bark every day.

• Every day a blue whale swallows four tonnes of tiny sea creatures called plankton – that's more food than a human eats in a year. Mind you, the whale is 2,000 times heavier than a human.

• Even tiny creatures can munch more for their size than humans. For example, the 2-gram Etruscan shrew scoffs up to three times its own weight every day. That's like a human eating one entire sheep, 50 chickens, 60 family-sized loaves and 150 apples every day. You'd never cram all that into your lunch box, would you? So why do the shrews stuff their little faces? Well, they have to. Shrews need the energy all this food gives them to keep active and warm in cold weather.

COULD YOU BE A SCIENTIST?

If you like food, you don't have to become a chef. You could become a scientist instead. Yes, scientists have performed some mouth-watering experiments. Can you predict the results?

1 In the 1970s a group of American scientists went to a party and watched people eating. (Don't do this at parties – it's rude.) The scientists found that overweight people ate more than thinner people. The scientists quickly grabbed the food and took it into another room. What happened next?
a) The overweight people went into the next room to get the food.
b) The overweight people couldn't be bothered to move. The thinner people went next door and helped themselves.
c) A fight broke out and the scientists were chucked out for spoiling the party.

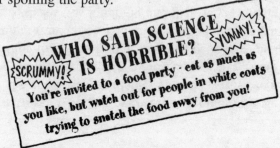

WHO SAID SCIENCE IS HORRIBLE?
SCRUMMY! YUMMY!
You're invited to a food party - eat as much as you like, but watch out for people in white coats trying to snatch the food away from you!

2 In the 1970s scientists at Virginia University, in America asked a group of people to sample a selection of yummy ice creams after first slurping down a rich, sweet milk-shake. (And this was a science experiment?!) The aim was to see which group ate the most ice cream.

What did they find?

a) People who were trying to lose weight ate more ice cream.

b) People who were trying to lose weight ate less ice cream.

c) Everyone scoffed as much as they could because the food was free and then threw up everywhere.

Answers: 1 b) The overweight people only ate more if the food was available. If food wasn't available, the thinner people ate more because they were more willing to go and find it. **2 a)** The people trying to lose weight were upset. The scientists had told them that the milk-shake was fattening and that they'd broken their diet. So they pigged out on ice cream because they felt they might as well enjoy themselves.

ENORMOUS APPETITES

The amount you can eat depends on how big your stomach is. After all, you've got to put all that food somewhere. This is also controlled by a pea-sized lump on the underside of the brain called the hypothalamus (hi-po-thala-mus). This signals to your brain when it's time to eat and when to stop. If you don't want to stop, then chances are that you're eating something you really enjoy. And if you don't want to start eating, then you're probably sitting in front of your school dinner…

FOUL FOOD FAVOURITES

Food is vital. It does more than simply fill you up. It supplies the chemicals that your body needs to stay healthy and grow. But we all have foods we love. And we all have foods we love to hate. Here's a school dinner menu. Which dishes might tempt you?

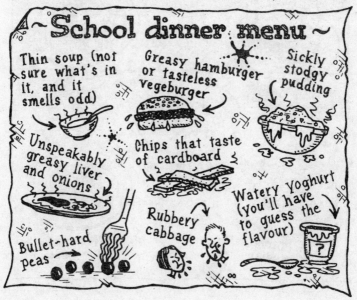

~ School dinner menu ~

Thin soup (not sure what's in it, and it smells odd)

Greasy hamburger or tasteless vegeburger

Sickly stodgy pudding

Unspeakably greasy liver and onions

Chips that taste of cardboard

Bullet-hard peas

Rubbery cabbage

Watery yoghurt (you'll have to guess the flavour)

It's really strange, but some teachers and even a few otherwise quite normal people think school dinners are the height of good taste! Because that's all a favourite food is – just a matter of taste. Like most people you probably chose your favourite foods when you were about two years old. But all over the world people enjoy different foods. Including some that might seem horrible to you. We managed to talk fearless Private Eye M I Gutzache into sampling a few of these foreign delicacies.

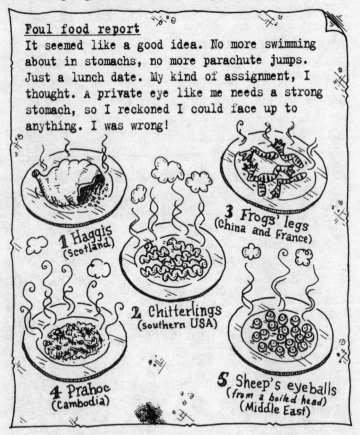

<u>Foul food report</u>
It seemed like a good idea. No more swimming about in stomachs, no more parachute jumps. Just a lunch date. My kind of assignment, I thought. A private eye like me needs a strong stomach, so I reckoned I could face up to anything. I was wrong!

1 Haggis (Scotland)

2 Chitterlings (southern USA)

3 Frogs' legs (China and France)

4 Prahoc (Cambodia)

5 Sheep's eyeballs (from a boiled head) (Middle East)

1. Tasted good – I like the savoury taste of onions and herbs and meat. I was just enjoying my second helping when someone mentioned that the meat was sheep's heart and lungs wrapped up in its stomach. I suddenly needed some fresh air.

2. This was really good. Nice crunchy batter. Then they told me it was chopped pigs intestines with corn meal fried in lard. I swallowed hard and went on to the next dish.

3. I could see what this dish was. I shut my eyes and took a bite. It tasted like watery chicken. I'd prefer chicken any day.

4. Tasted a bit fishy. No, I don't mean fishy suspicious – just fishy and kind of salty. But when I learned the fish had been squashed to paste and left to rot for a few days, I decided they could keep their rotten fish.

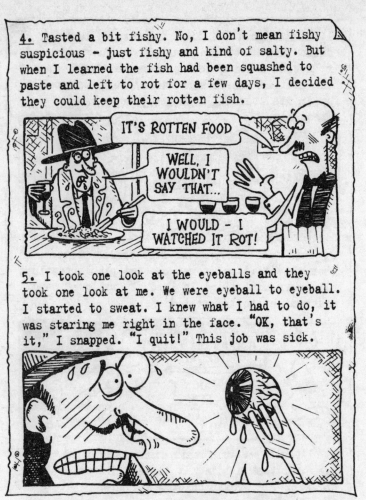

5. I took one look at the eyeballs and they took one look at me. We were eyeball to eyeball. I started to sweat. I knew what I had to do, it was staring me right in the face. "OK, that's it," I snapped. "I quit!" This job was sick.

Poor old Gutzache, he couldn't cope with the eyeball because he wasn't used to eating that part of an animal. But if he eats tongue, breast and neck, what difference does an eyeball make? It's all a question of what you're used to. If Gutzache had grown up in the Middle East he'd have been eating eyeballs since he was two – and loving them!

And here's something else you shouldn't try.

POISON PILLS

Some people will eat just about anything. But would you believe that some people used to eat poison? In 1733 dangerously dodgy doctor Ned Ward sold antimony pills as a cure for everything including upset tummies. But antimony is a poison once used by the ancient Egyptians to bump off flies. So not surprisingly the pills caused

violent stomach pains. One joker wrote a poem about
Ned Ward:

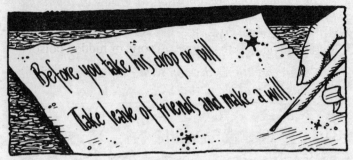

Before you take his drop or pill
Take leave of friends and make a will.

But most people believed the adverts and thought
the pain was part of the cure. The doctor made his
fortune. He even gave poor sick people free samples of
the wonderful pills. How kind! But oddly enough Ward
never tried his own pills. This may explain why he lived
to a ripe old age.

But antimony is just one of a host of disgusting
poisons that turn up in food. Watch out, the next chapter
could give you a nasty reaction...

FATAL FOOD POISONING

Food can be fatal. Well, not the food itself but what's lurking inside it. There may be all sorts of hidden poisons and germs lying in wait for your unsuspecting innards. So in order to protect yourself, you need to know all the disgusting details.

Disgusting digestion fact file

NAME: Poisons

THE BASIC FACTS: A poison is a chemical that gets into your body and makes you sick. Poisons include acids that dissolve the guts. Other poisons get to the brain in the bloodstream and knock the victim out.

THE HORRIBLE DETAILS: 1 Some of the deadliest poisons are called toxins. They're made by germs that get into food. Some can kill.

2 The best way for your body to get rid of a poison is to throw it back up again. That's why people spend the whole night throwing up after eating a dodgy dinner that's alive with germs.

BARF!

41

TEACHER'S TEA-BREAK TEASER

Try this teaser during a teacher's tea break. It'll be as welcome as a snail in a salad bar. Tap lightly on the staffroom door. When the door creaks open your teacher will be holding the regulation mug of sludgy mud-coloured coffee. Smile sweetly and say:

I WAS JUST WONDERING IF COFFEE IS A POISON AND IF SO HOW MUCH YOU NEED TO DRINK BEFORE IT KILLS YOU?

ERK!

Answer: Coffee can be poisonous if you drink too much too fast. It contains a chemical called caffeine (also found in tea and cola drinks) that makes the heart beat faster. Normally it's quite harmless but scientists reckon that if someone drank 100 cups in four hours the caffeine would be strong enough to put their heart and blood vessels under fatal pressure.

SOME GOOD AND SOME BAD NEWS

Here's the good news: it's not easy to get poisoned. As long as you're sensible about what you put in your mouth, you're not going to get poisoned by man-made chemicals. If it isn't a drink don't drink it, and if it isn't food don't eat it. And food poisoning caused by germs is fairly rare, too.

Now the bad news: crowds of germs hang around in the hope of causing some really foul food poisoning. At best these awful invaders cause an upset tummy. At worst they can kill – as you'll discover in the next chapter.

So what does food poisoning do to you? We've managed to get hold of a doctor's notes on a case of food poisoning. See if you can decipher the doctor's dodgy handwriting.

THE CASE OF THE POISON PORK PIE

The patient is in great distress. He's a teacher at Gunge Street School and says he ate an ancient pork pie in the school canteen. He now has pain in the intestines and is vomiting every half-hour and he's producing diarrhoea (runny faeces). I believe that the muscles of the patient's gut are squeezing all the food and water out of each end. The patient's body is trying to get rid of infected food.

DIAGNOSIS: The patient has food poisoning

TREATMENT: The patient needs complete rest from school for a few days. For the first day or two he should drink only flat lemonade or warm water with a pinch of sugar and salt. This should stop his body drying out or dehydrating, whilst the white blood cells from his blood move into the gut and eat up the remaining germs.

PROGNOSIS: He'll live to bite another day.

Yes, germs are always ready to attack us. As you'll find out on page 48, our favourite private eye M I Gutzache is hot on the trail of the germs. But the germs are hatching their own dastardly plans...

Right lads, our enemy is the entire human race. Your mission is to get into their food and drink and raid their guts. Your orders are to make 'em sick. Make 'em throw up, and make 'em really miserable. You will start your mission as soon as the fridge door opens. Read these plans carefully and then eat them. Good luck, lads!

TOP SECRET BATTLE PLANS ~
KEEP OUT OF REACH OF HUMANS

1 GO UNDER COVER IMMEDIATELY

Good hiding places: soil, dirty water. Humans won't dare look for you there. Lumps of dung or rubbish bins provide even better cover.

SOIL   DIRTY WATER   DUNG   RUBBISH

2 GET MOBILE

Your first objective: get on a human's hands and fingers and clothes and then onto their food. Human fingernails provide excellent shelter, and they'll do the job for you. You'll be inside the body in no time!

A fly can offer first-class aerial support. Aim to be picked up from a cowpat when the fly drops in to suck up moisture. The fly will then proceed to rendezvous with human food. The fly sicks its digestive juices over the food and sucks up the mixture. Now's your chance to drop onto the food.

FLY

COWPAT

HUMAN FOOD

GNASH! MUNCH! SUCK! SQUIRT! GUZZLE!

3 GET STUCK IN

Start eating. Squirt out enzymes that turn the food into slime and suck it into your body. Be sure to make plenty of waste chemicals to make the food rotten and stinking.

SAUSAGE BEFORE   SAUSAGE AFTER

4 GET NEW RECRUITS

Another simple task: pull yourself in half. Again and again. Soon you'll have hundreds, then thousands and millions of reinforcements. This will provide overwhelming numbers for the big attack on the guts.

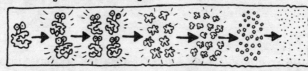

5 A FINAL WARNING

Humans will try to fight back with every weapon at their disposal. Be on your guard for antibiotics – medicines made from chemicals that us germs produce to defend ourselves against rival germs. And watch out. If a human uses enough antibiotics your entire army could be wiped out.

MESSAGE TO ALL GERMS
KEEP AWAY FROM ANTIBIOTICS

45

Dare you discover … how things rot?

You will need:
A freshly cut piece of orange
A large polythene bag
An adult helper

What you do:
Place the orange in the bag and seal the bag tightly so that no air can escape. Leave the bag in a warm place for six days.
What do you notice?
a) The orange stays the same.
b) The orange goes mushy and smelly.
c) The orange grows bigger.

Answer: b) Germs have been feeding on the orange and slowly digesting it and making a foul pong. The germs may be harmful, so don't open the bag – throw it away unopened!

HOW NOT TO HANDLE FOOD
Here are some sure-fire ways to give germs a helping hand into your food…
• Sneezing into food.

• Coughing into food. This shoots germs from your mouth and nose into the air. Use a handkerchief. Do not wrap your food in the handkerchief or use it as a bandage afterwards. Germs can also get into your body through unwashed wounds.

• Handling food without washing your hands. (There are usually a few germs hanging around on your hands.)
• Picking your nose or biting nails. This is a marvellous way to pick up a few million germs. It's especially anti-social if you try to do both at the same time.

• Picking bits of food from your teeth with your fingers and then eating it. Not recommended.

DISGUSTING DETECTIVE WORK

Following the sad case of the food-poisoned teacher (see page 43), we decided to investigate the school kitchen that was suspected of foul play and even fouler pork pies. It needed someone with experience, with dedication and above all … with guts. There was only one man for a case like this…

FOUL FOOD REPORT by M I Gutzache

At last, some real detective work! Something undercover. I'd heard that school kitchens were clean places that were inspected regularly by public health officers. But this one was different. It proved a real dirty business. Stomach churning, in fact, but I got the pictures in the end.

Can you spot the germ danger signs in each picture?

FRESH FOOD QUIZ

If cooks manage to get rid of bacteria they can keep food fresh for longer. Which of the following methods will work?

1 Boiling food and sealing it in an air-tight container.
2 Squashing the food and germs into a plastic box.
3 Mixing the food with lots of sugar or salt.

4 Smoking the food over a really smoky fire.

5 Sucking all the air out of the food so the bacteria can't breathe.

6 Freezing the food with the bacteria in it.

7 Drying the food out so the bacteria can't drink.

8 Spinning the food around really fast. The germs get so dizzy that they die.

Answers: 1 Yes. Any thorough heating, as in cooking, will kill bacteria. Keeping food in an air-tight container such as the cans you buy in a supermarket will stop bacteria from getting back in. **2 No.** The bacteria will still live and breed, and destroy the food. **3 Yes.** The sugar draws water from the food and the bacteria can't live without water. That's why jam doesn't go rotten. **4 Yes.** The smoke covers the food with chemicals such as nitrites that kill the bacteria. This is what keeps smoked fish such as kippers fresh. **5 Yes.** This is what happens when food is vacuum packed. The food will keep in this form for months. **6 Yes.** The cold kills the bacteria. That's why food stays fresh in the freezer. **7 Yes.** The bacteria can survive as tiny seeds called spores, but drying out stops them from being active. **8 No.** Bacteria don't get dizzy.

We've painted a pretty grim picture of the germ world and maybe we're being a bit unfair. After all, they're just doing what comes naturally – for a germ that is. And we can't get rid of germs altogether. There are different germs in different countries and some will always manage to get into our bodies. Then our bodies have to fight against the disgusting, deadly digestive diseases that are lurking in the next chapter. BEWARE!

DEADLY DIGESTIVE DISEASES

If there's something even more disgusting than digestion then it's the dreadful digestive diseases that germs can cause. There's a long, horrible list of them and many are not just disgusting, they're deadly, too. We asked our Private Eye M I Gutzache to compile a dossier on the worst villains. Gunge Street School was in trouble. More teachers and some children too were going down with dangerous diseases. The kitchens needed inspection, there were various germs under suspicion. Gutzache was ready for the job.

A DEADLY GERM DOSSIER

by MI Gutzache

They're a real mean bunch of no-good low-lifes. Even I was shocked at the things these guys get up to. I shuddered to think they were hiding out in the very school kitchen I'd visited. These germs hit the young and the old hardest. That's bad news for young kids and tired old teachers. These germs must be stopped before they close down the school.

NAME: Salmonella
KNOWN HAUNTS: A real shady character - hides out in raw meat and eggs. Its favourite bolt-holes are chicken guts. I saw a chicken in the fridge at Gunge Street. It didn't look too healthy.
ALIASES: Over 1,000 varieties - just take your pick.
KNOWN CRIMES: Causes repeated vomiting and diarrhoea. Responsible for hundreds of thousands of attacks all over the world. A killer.

NAME: Listeria
KNOWN HAUNTS: Soil, dung, dirty water, cheese, chicken or salads. I've got my doubts about the cheese at Gunge Street. It smelt kind of prehistoric. The germ's known to be at home at -5°C (24°F). So putting the cheese in the fridge won't do

much good. This character is tough – it can even live at 42°C (106°F). If a human got that hot they'd need a doctor fast.

KNOWN CRIMES: Causes violent sickness. These germs could spoil your whole day.

NAME: Staphylococcus

KNOWN HAUNTS: Nostrils, on skin especially in cuts and boils. The Gunge Street cooks must have been crawling with these germs. The germs hang out on food that should be kept in the fridge but that's been left out too long. Like the awful-smelling Gunge Street mince that was left out mouldering for three whole days.

MODE OF OPERATION: Gets on to food from un-bandaged cuts on hands.

KNOWN CRIMES: Causes diarrhoea, vomiting and painful cramps in the guts. These germs could spoil your whole week.

NAME: Clostridium botulinum

CAUSES: Botulism

KNOWN HAUNTS: Soil, fish, meat and vegetables.

MODE OF OPERATION: Thankfully no one's seen this germ at Gunge Street.

KNOWN CRIMES: Botulism causes double vision, weakness, difficulty talking and . . . DEATH.

WEAPONS: The toxin produced by this germ is deadly. Just 10mg could poison every human on Earth.

Conclusion

These guys are bad news. They must be rounded up. But it's going to be a tough job. They're a big mob and they've got so many hideouts. There's just one weapon that'll get them beat – and that's cleanliness!

But some germs are much more deadly and hopefully we'll never come across these criminal characters in Gunge Street kitchens ...

USEFUL WEAPONS

NAME: Vibrio cholerae

CAUSES: Cholera

KNOWN HAUNTS: Water mixed with faeces from another cholera sufferer.

MODE OF OPERATION: Gets into the body through eating shellfish that live in this dirty water. (Must be careful next time I eat oysters.) More usually spread by drinking the dirty water itself.

Drinking water sounded like a real dumb move. So I checked out the local water company and they said they had the problem sussed. They put chlorine in the water to blow the germs away.

KNOWN CRIMES: Causes violent vomiting, deadly diarrhoea and painful cramps. The victim's body dries out and turns blue. You could easily wake up to find yourself DEAD.

CHOLERA VICTIM

NAME: Salmonella typhi
CAUSES: Typhoid
KNOWN HAUNTS: The faeces of someone who has had the disease and survived. Typhoid is a relative of the notorious salmonella crime family.
MODE OF OPERATION: Gets around on dust or flies or dirty fingers.
KNOWN CRIMES: Causes a rash and a nasty cough. Turns the victim's faeces into a green and runny soup. If untreated it kills 20 per cent of its victims. Hey, that's nasty!

NAME: Shigella dysenteriae
CAUSES: Dysentery
KNOWN HAUNTS: The guts and faeces, dirty water and food.
KNOWN ALIASES: Can be caused by amoeba – the scientist guy says that's a microscopic blob-like animal. I'll take his word for it.
KNOWN CRIMES: Spreads from the guts to the liver and causes a deadly fever. It can even make holes in the gut.

Conclusion

I'm feeling sick. During my mission to the school kitchen I came over kind of hungry. Figured a piece of fruit wouldn't do any harm – now I've got pains in my gut and I'm feeling feverish. It's dysentry . . . I'm sure of it. ARGHH my guts! QUICK – where's the bathroom?

Bet you never knew!
Dysentery can be deadly for doctors even if they don't catch the disease. In the year AD580 Queen Austrechild, wife of King Guntram of the Franks had the disease really badly. She was tended by two doctors. Half-crazed with fever, she thought they were trying to poison her. So she made her grief-stricken husband promise that if she died the doctors would be executed. She died – and the unlucky doctors got the chop.

Over 1,000 years later one man was determined to stamp out the curse of dysentery and all the other deadly digestive diseases.

Hall of fame: Louis Pasteur (1822–1895)
Nationality: French

Louis Pasteur had embarrassing table manners. He would fiddle with his bread. He'd tear a slice into crumbs and inspect them for dust and wool and bits of cockroaches. If he found anything suspicious he would examine it at the table using a portable microscope. (Don't start getting ideas now!)

57

Next Pasteur would study the glasses. He'd wipe away tiny specks of dirt that no one else could see. And if that wasn't bad enough he'd launch into a loud and detailed account of his latest gruesome experiments with mice or bits of mashed-up body and germs. This was because Louis Pasteur was obsessed with germs. He was so desperate to keep germs off his hands that he wouldn't shake hands with anyone. But oddly enough Mrs Pasteur didn't complain about her husband's habits. She was his most devoted helper.

Louis Pasteur was the deadliest enemy the germ world ever had. He hunted germs like a determined cop hunts a master criminal. With a total and ruthless dedication he worked weekends and evenings – refusing to give up ever. But then Pasteur had every reason to hate germs. Two of his children had died of typhoid.

At school no one thought young Louis was especially clever. His teachers said he was "passable" at physics and "mediocre" at chemistry. But Louis stuck at his science studies and eventually became a Professor of Chemistry. These are just a few of his achievements:

• He proved that germs make wine and beer go sour. This work involved going to vineyards and sampling wines (all in the interests of science, of course). Pasteur discovered that if you heat liquids to 72°C (161°F) for a few seconds you can kill germs without spoiling the taste. He had invented pasteurisation – which is used today to stop your milk going off too quickly.

• He went on holiday leaving a mix of chicken cholera germs and broth. (Chickens suffer a different type of cholera to humans.) When he got back he found that many of the germs had died. He gave the mixture of weakened germs to some chickens and found they stayed healthy. The chickens' bodies had produced chemical defences against the dead germs that they could use to fight living germs. We call the dead germs a vaccine and it's what you get when you're vaccinated against a disease.

COME ON, DON'T BE A CHICKEN . . . I MEAN DON'T BE SCARED.

• Pasteur went on to develop vaccines against the killer diseases anthrax and rabies. The rabies vaccine was particularly welcome because rabies *always* kills its victims. Trouble is, the rabies vaccine has to be delivered by painful injections, but at least the victim gets to live.

COULD YOU BE A SCIENTIST?

In 1860 Pasteur climbed a mountain carrying sealed flasks containing yeast extract broth and sugar. At 1,500 metres (5,000 feet) he opened the flasks and filled them with cold mountain air then re-sealed them. Pasteur believed that the broth would only go off if germs from the air could get to it. He had already filled other flasks with air from the top of one hill, then another higher hill, and a cellar. What were the results?

a) All the flasks showed the same amount of germs. This proved that germs are found at all heights.

b) The most germs were found up the mountain and on the higher hill. This is because the wind blows germs up in the air.

c) The most germs were on the lower hill. The least germs were found up the mountain and in the cellar.

Answer: c) Pasteur proved that germs spread on specks of dust. The cellar was well sealed so the dust couldn't get in easily and the mountain air had even less dust so there were fewer germs. The germs couldn't get into the sealed flasks and their contents stayed fresh. In fact, one of the flasks from 1860 is now a museum exhibit and the broth is still fresh … anyone want to try it?

TYPHOID MARCHES ON...

Despite Pasteur's hard work he couldn't trace the deadly germ that had killed his children. The typhoid germ was eventually tracked down by Karl Joseph Eberth (1835–1926) in 1880. But the disease continued to claim lives. Edith Claypole (1870–1915), a talented American scientist, died of the disease in 1915. She was in the middle of a study of ... typhoid fever. And in 1909 doctors faced the killer disease again. Here are the facts in a story that tells how they might have happened.

TYPHOID MARY

New York, 1909

Mary Mallon was a killer and her lethal weapon was ice cream. Delicious, home-made ice cream. But could it really kill people? Guns or bombs, maybe – but ice cream?

And Mary didn't look dangerous. She was a shy woman of about 40 years of age with grey hair tied neatly in a bun. She wore small round spectacles and her plump figure seemed an excellent advertisement for her wholesome cooking. No wonder Dr George Soper felt confused as he stood in the kitchen in Park Avenue.

Surely Mary wouldn't harm a fly?

Then the doctor noticed Mary's hands. Big red raw hands that were used to hard kitchen work – hands that hadn't been washed in a week. They weren't just dirty – they were filthy. Every hollow and vein and knuckle was smeared with grime, and there was thick, black dirt under her fingernails.

"Well, sir, why did you want to see me?" she asked in her soft Irish voice. "I haven't got all day. The people here are taken badly. The daughter is dead and the servants are sick. I've lots to do."

The doctor pulled himself together. He had difficult and unpleasant things to say. "Mary Mallon, I have reason to believe you are spreading an infectious and fatal disease."

Mary didn't even blink. It was as if the doctor had said something about the weather.

"I don't know what you're talking about, sir," she said quietly.

"Let me explain," said the doctor. "Last year you worked as a cook at Oyster Bay, Long Island. Six people in that house fell sick with typhoid fever."

"So they got sick. People do – what's that to me?" asked Mary sounding a bit more annoyed.

"I talked to the family and I checked what they ate. The family all said they enjoyed eating ice cream. Your ice cream that you always make by hand."

Mary's mouth drooped crossly at the corners and she slowly pulled open a drawer under the table.

"You've had eight jobs in seven years," continued the doctor grimly. "And in seven of those eight houses there have been cases of typhoid fever."

Mary's filthy fingers groped for the meat cleaver.

"Mary," said the doctor coldly, "I think the typhoid was spread on your dirty hands."

"ARRRGGGGH!" With a banshee wail Mary threw herself on the doctor. She screamed in fury, "I'll learn ye. You meddling doctor – I'll chop ye up for sausages. I'll have ye for breakfast. I'LL KILL YE!"

Dr Soper leapt sideways just in time. The heavy cleaver hacked into the table top. He tore round the kitchen chased by Mary brandishing her weapon.

Dr Soper escaped and gasped out his story to New

York's Chief of Police. The police moved in swiftly. They raided Mary's house and found her hiding in an outside toilet. It took seven policemen to carry her shrieking and wailing to a waiting ambulance.

A few months later at the Riverside Hospital for Communicable Diseases in New York, Dr Soper sat in his office a little uneasily. The time had come for a talk with Mary. Or "Typhoid Mary" as the newspapers were now calling her.

"Typhoid is a terrible disease," began the doctor. "You get fever, spots, stomach pains, a cough and bowel movements that look like pea soup. But you'll remember all that, won't you Mary?"

"Why should I remember anything?" asked Mary grumpily. She glared up at Dr Soper's two hefty assistants who stood either side of her. Ready for the first sign of trouble.

Dr Soper sighed, "Our tests prove that you've had the disease. Although you got better, the germs are still in your gall bladder. They pass out of your body every time you visit the toilet. Some germs get on your hands and if you don't wash them they also get onto food."

"I don't understand," moaned Mary, "I'm a cook. I do me job but no one tells me nothing."

Then Dr Soper offered his reluctant patient a choice. She could give up cooking or she could stay locked up in the island hospital. For ever.

"You can't keep me here," protested Mary. "Why are you doing this to me?"

Dr Soper grimly shook his head. "Oh, but we can keep you here, Mary. We have the legal power. But you do have another choice. Allow us to cut out your gall-bladder. It's a risky operation, but you'll be free of germs after we've done it. And then we'll let you go."

"I'll kill ye!" spat Mary struggling with the two assistants. "I'll never let ye near me gall-bladder – whatever that is."

But three years later Mary had a change of heart. Not about the operation, though. She agreed to give up cooking and report to Dr Soper every three months. But after she left the hospital she promptly disappeared.

In 1915 an epidemic of typhoid fever hit New York's Sloane Hospital for Women. Two members of staff died. One morning the kitchen maid was having a laugh with a friend. "That old cook, Mrs Brown," she sniggered, "she's so grumpy and guess what? She looks just like that woman in the papers a few years ago. What's-her-name – Typhoid Mary!"

Listening at the door, the cook, who was really Mary Mallon, clenched her dirty fists in rage.

Once again Mary disappeared but this time the police were on her trail. She was arrested soon afterwards. Mary Mallon had knowingly spread typhoid and people had died. How do you think she was punished?

a) Mary Mallon was executed for murder. The judge said: "Mary, you are too dangerous to live."

b) Mary was drugged by Dr Soper and while she was unconscious he removed her gall bladder. When she was completely free of typhoid germs the doctors let her go.

c) Mary was never released. She was locked up on the island for the rest of her life.

Answer: c) Mary was never released. She was the first known carrier of typhoid fever and although she was never charged with a crime she was judged a menace to public health. In 1923 the doctors built her a cottage in the hospital grounds and gave her a job working in the hospital lab that studied germs – such as typhoid.

Today Mary Mallon is world famous as "Typhoid Mary." All she ever wanted to do was to make ice cream. But her name is linked for ever to a disease she never truly understood.

THE FIGHT GOES ON

Louis Pasteur's work showed scientists how to discover germs and how to develop new drugs and vaccines to combat them. Today doctors cure typhoid using drugs. Meanwhile, the world-wide battle against other diseases continues. For example, in the 1970s 4,000,000 children a year were dying of cholera. In 1974 World Health Organization scientists invented a drink made from clean water, minerals and sugar which can be given to cholera victims to stop them drying out. This simple drink, named ORT (oral re-hydration therapy), has saved the lives of thousands of children.

So that's the answer. If we can keep germs at bay we can all live happily ever after. Er, no. Here comes the really bad news. Eating clean food can make you ill! Some people even die from their diets! Will you be able to stomach the next chapter? Better read on and find out...

A HORRIBLY HEALTHY DIET

There's a lot more to food than meets the eye. There are loads of vital ingredients that you must have in your daily diet. To find out more we persuaded Private Eye M I Gutzache to sneak back into the school kitchens to collect samples. At first he said he couldn't face going back to that revolting place. But after a bit of bribery and gentle persuasion with a roll of banknotes he dragged himself off his sick bed.

GUTZACHE GOES INTO ... SCHOOL DINNERS

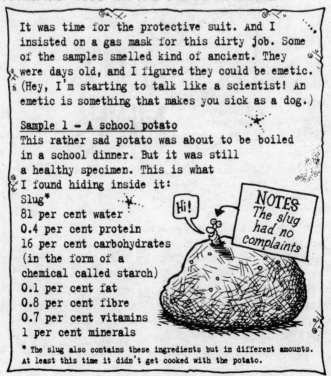

It was time for the protective suit. And I insisted on a gas mask for this dirty job. Some of the samples smelled kind of ancient. They were days old, and I figured they could be emetic. (Hey, I'm starting to talk like a scientist! An emetic is something that makes you sick as a dog.)

Sample 1 - A school potato
This rather sad potato was about to be boiled in a school dinner. But it was still a healthy specimen. This is what I found hiding inside it:
Slug*
81 per cent water
0.4 per cent protein
16 per cent carbohydrates
(in the form of a
chemical called starch)
0.1 per cent fat
0.8 per cent fibre
0.7 per cent vitamins
1 per cent minerals

Hi!

NOTES
The slug had no complaints

* The slug also contains these ingredients but in different amounts. At least this time it didn't get cooked with the potato.

Sample 2 - A glass of water

NOTES Useful for washing taste of dinner away

STRAY PEA

GREASY FINGER PRINTS

It wasn't much to look at, but my investigation revealed that you need about two litres of this clear runny stuff every day. Half of this comes from water in your food (like the watery potato), and half from what you actually drink. You've got to top up your water supply 'cos your body is two-thirds water and bits such as your brain are 80 per cent water. So you know what'll happen if you don't drink enough of it - pea-brain!

Sample 3 - Jam pudding

This pudding is oozing with sticky sugar. It looked good enough to eat, but the news was bad.

SUGAR

NOTES Just looking at it gave me toothache

The scientist guy says sugar gives you the energy your body needs but nothing else. He says I eat more sugar than my body needs. Seems there's enough sugar rolling around inside me to fill a jam jar. I was chewing a candy bar at the time. I put it down and decided I'd had enough sugar for one day. Only a scientist could spoil my appetite.

Bet you never knew!

Sugar hangs out in loads of savoury foods, too – just a small tin of baked beans contains two to three teaspoonfuls of sugar. And you'll find it in cereals, tinned meat, soup, tinned vegetables, peanut butter and even coleslaw. Sweet foods have even more sugar – a chocolate bar has ten teaspoonfuls. Most of us probably get through 30 teaspoonfuls of sugar a day. Wow!

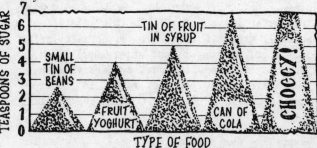

Sample 4 – Mashed swede

Hidden inside this strange and tasteless lump of orange vegetable I came across a strange and tasteless food chemical. It's called starch, a type of carbohydrate the same as I found in that potato. It's made out of sugar chemicals joined in a chain. The scientists say that inside your muscles enzymes can rip apart the sugar chemicals and free the energy to help your body move. Sounds good – why did it have to taste so bad?

Sample 5 – School dinner chips

The chips were cold and greasy and oozing with fat. They hang around in your stomach like a sack of cement. The fats stay down longer than most foods and at least they make you feel nice and full. But it seems spare fat turns into body fat slopping lazily around your stomach and backside. And get this – there's usually enough fat in your body at any one time to make seven bars of soap!

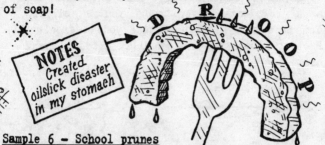

NOTES
Created oilslick disaster in my stomach

Sample 6 – School prunes

Hmm, prunes. Can't say I liked the taste, they had a weird kind of leathery texture. But my investigation showed that's 'cos they're loaded with fibre. That's the stuff that makes brown bread chewy and fruit and veg stringy. Seems your body can't digest fibre but it keeps the rest of your food moving in the gut. The gut walls can grip the fibre more easily than ordinary food. In the end this gets moving, too ... to the bathroom.

Sample 7 – Smelly cheese

NOTES
Relieved to find the smell wasn't from my socks

Some of the kids I interviewed had strange ideas about where the cheese came from. Well, I wasn't here to find out about its past – I was looking for the inside story and I found it. Cheese is

25 per cent protein - your body uses this substance to build muscles. Although your body is 20 per cent protein you don't need tonnes of the stuff. If you're 12 years old you need about 45 grams of protein a day. That's as much as a as a grown woman, even though you're smaller. You need more protein because you're growing. Protein also hangs out in milk, cheese, fish, meat, beans and nuts.

NOTES
I've sketched some useful sources of protein

Sample 8 - Suspect salt

All this suspect food had got to me. A cold bead of sweat trickled down my face. I tried to lick it off. Ugh - salt! Try it yourself - that's what sweat contains. We use salt for killing germs and, as I found, it comes in handy for disguising the vile taste of school dinners. There are 14,000 different uses for salt - but I've got a report to finish, so I'm not going to list them all here.

Salt is vital for many of the chemical reactions that go on in your body. Sweating is one way your body gets rid of any spare salt. But salt isn't the only mineral you've just gotta have.

MYSTERIOUS MINERALS

The school dinner samples were loaded with mysterious minerals. They're vital in tiny amounts for building your body and making useful chemicals.

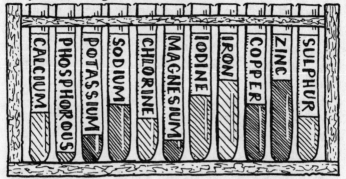

You might be amazed to learn that your school dinner contains all these strange and foul-smelling chemicals. Oh – you aren't? Well, your teacher might be...

TEST YOUR TEACHER

Try testing your teacher or even your school cook (if you dare) on this fascinating topic.

1 Sulphur is a foul-tasting chemical but it makes up 0.25 per cent of your body. How much sulphur is that?
a) Enough to kill all the fleas on a dog.
b) Enough to kill all the fleas on an elephant.
c) Enough to kill all the fleas on a rat.
2 Iron is a vital mineral that your body uses to give blood it's brilliant red colour. What happens when you don't eat enough?
a) Your blood turns yellow.
b) You come out in spots and a fever.
c) You become pale and tired and don't feel like eating.

3 Your body is 0.004 per cent iron (lucky it doesn't rust!). How much iron is that?

a) Enough to make the head of a pin.

b) Enough to make a 5-cm nail.

c) Enough to make an iron lump the size of your arm bone.

4 Calcium is a vital raw material for bones. A 12-year-old child needs 700 mg of calcium a day. What's that equal to?

a) Four plates of spinach.

b) 40 plates of spinach. (Yuck!)

c) No spinach because this vegetable doesn't contain calcium.

5 What's the best source of iodine?

a) Rainwater

b) Snails

c) Seaweed

GETTING IT IN THE NECK

You only need 0.004 grams of iodine every day. But without it life is a pain in the neck. Here's why.

Iodine comes from the sea – that's why seaweed has so much of it. The iodine gets blown inshore as sea spray and collects on plants.

You eat them. A special part of your neck called the thyroid gland uses the iodine to make a chemical called thyroxine (thi-rox-een). Thyroxine makes your body grow and use up food faster.

Without enough iodine the thyroid gland swells up as it tries to filter every last drop of the mineral from your blood. It forms a hideous lump called a goitre (goy-ter).

In the 1800s part of the mid-west USA furthest from the sea was known as the "goitre belt". There was less iodine there so, of course, more people developed goitres.

You'll find lots of iodine in seafood, fish and, of course, seaweed (if you can face eating it).

COULD YOU BE A SCIENTIST?

This disgusting experiment is common in university science courses. The aim is to show how thyroxine works. Take one harmless little bull-frog tadpole. It can take up to two years to turn into a frog. Feed it one drop of thyroxine. What happens next?

a) The tadpole turns into a frog.

b) The tadpole turns into a giant tadpole.

c) The tadpole grows a goitre.

Answer: a) Within a few hours the thyroxine turns the tadpole into a tiny frog the size of your little fingernail. Sadly, when the other tadpoles become frogs they're 100 times bigger. And given half a chance they'll gobble up their tiny brother or sister.

VITAL VITAMINS

Vitamins aren't an optional extra. They're vital chemicals that keep you healthy. They're so important that you can buy lots of different pills and drinks that aim to provide extra vitamins. The adverts are everywhere:

Vit·A

Carrot-cocktail-Slurp

Do you suffer from spots? Having trouble shaking off the dandruff? Can't see in the dark? You could be missing out on vitamin A. Vit A Carrot-Cocktail-Slurp is the obvious answer.

Just one slurp and you'll be spotting black cats in coal cellars! Yes that lovely vitamin A makes a chemical called visual purple at the back of the eye, so helping your eyes to see better in poor light.

BEFORE

AFTER

THE SMALL PRINT
You CAN get too much of a good thing. Drink too much Vit A Vita-Slurp and your hair will fall out and you could die. Yes DIE. Too much vitamin A can poison you which is why people can die if they eat a vitamin A-rich polar-bear liver.

Ingredients: extract of liver, milk, butter, eggs, fish and carrots.*

*That's why people say that carrots help you see in the dark.

Vit B

Get-up-and-go-Slurp

Tired and run-down? You need Vit B Get-up-and-go-Slurp! Why not try all eight mouth-watering varieties?

B3 "B5" B6" B7
"B2" B8
B1 B12"

BEFORE   **AFTER**

Just one slurp and you'll be back on your feet. Yes, these vital vitamins help your body turn food into energy. Healthy nerves and blood guaranteed.

Ingredients: extracts of wholemeal bread, yeast extract, milk, nuts and fresh vegetables.

THE SMALL PRINT
Lack of vitamin B5 makes a rat's fur go grey. But humans go grey anyway. And not even Vita-Slurp can stop it.

78

Vit D Sunny-Slurp

▶ Do your fingernails break at awkward moments?
▶ Are you getting enough vitamin D a day?
▶ One slurp of Vit D Sunny-Slurp and you'll be D-LIGHTED!

FANTASTIC!

Your tough fingernails will be the envy of your friends and you'll be proud of your strong bones and gleaming healthy teeth. Ingredients: Extracts of oil from a cod's liver, milk and cheese.*

THE SMALL PRINT
Don't let the delicious taste of this Slurp make you drink too much. Overdose on Vit D and you'll be sick and constipated (unable to produce poo).

*The body also makes vitamin D from the sunlight that falls on the skin.

Vit E
Suppleskin-Slurp

Drink Vita-Slurp A brand new range of vitamin drinks. A slurp-a-day keeps the doctor away!

BEFORE

AFTER!

Do you have tired sagging skin? Are there strange brown marks, or liver spots, on your hands? You need a shot of Vit E Suppleskin-Slurp. In no time you'll be glowing with good health and your body cells and blood system will heal damage more quickly.

Ingredients: extracts of vegetable oils, nuts and cereals.

> **THE SMALL PRINT**
> Some people have baths in Vit E Suppleskin-Slurp in a bid to stay young-looking. But this is going too far – it doesn't work – sorry!

Vit K
Kwik-clot Slurp

Drink Vita-Slurp A brand new range of vitamin drinks. A slurp-a-day keeps the doctor away!

Are you having trouble with clots? (No, not stupid people – we mean *blood* clots.) When you cut yourself, do you just keep bleeding? Essential for those more serious wounds, Vit K Kwik-clot Slurp will help your blood to clot-a-lot, so it stays where it belongs – that's inside your body, and not all over the carpet!

Ingredients: extracts of green vegetables and liver, and germs from the human gut!

IT'S SO ANNOYING!

BUT NOT ANY MORE

80

OK – got the message? Missing out on vitamins makes you sick. But it took doctors many years to discover which foods were the best sources of which vitamins. Here's the story of one man's search for the truth about the most horrible sickness of all – scurvy.

THE TERROR OF THE SEA

Stinking bad breath, swollen purple gums, easy bruising, wounds not healing, bleeding eyeballs, tiredness and death. Yep. Scurvy was no picnic. A few hundred years ago you could walk round any port and spot the sickly seafarers a mile off. They were the ones with no teeth.

But why did sailors suffer from scurvy more than other people? For sailors in the 18th and early 19th centuries it wasn't just the sea that was rough, life on board ship was pretty rough, too. Conditions were really grim and scurvy used to be the terror of the sea. Sailors feared catching scurvy more than shipwrecks, pirates or shark attacks. But for years no one knew what caused this terrible disease.

But some captains thought they knew…

And, of course, the captains had their favourite cures…

Ship's doctor James Lind (1716–1794) felt sure these cures were useless. But he had to prove it. He reckoned that the disgusting food on board ship was part of the problem. In the days before fridges and freezers it was impossible to keep food fresh at sea. So a typical meal looked like this.

1 HARD TACK AND MAGGOTS.*

2 WATER THAT STANK LIKE A BLOCKED TOILET.

3 STALE CHEESE WITH MORE MAGGOTS.

4 SALTY BACON.**

5 GREASY RANCID BUTTER

*A dried biscuit so hard that a London museum has a 200-year-old example. You had to tap your hard tack before you ate it to get the maggots out.
**It was so salty that it made you thirsty enough to drink the disgusting water.

But which of these foul foods caused scurvy? Or maybe as the food was so horrible, the seafarers were missing out on something in their diet. Perhaps they were getting the disease because of something they *weren't* eating.

Here's how James Lind might have written up his research:

HMS Salisbury, somewhere in the English Channel, 1747.

It's so frustrating. Here I am with 12 sailors sick with scurvy. I'm sure they're missing something in their diet - but what? I can't watch them die - I'm the doctor, I've got to try something. I'll have to experiment. I've always wanted to be a scientist. I'll divide the sailors into pairs and get each pair to try a cure suggested by other doctors. One of them has to work! Here goes!!

Sailors Walker Planke and Spike de Gunn will get a few drops of sulphuric acid a day. (Note: Mustn't make it too strong or it'll dissolve their guts.)

I'll give Davy Jones-Locker and Andy Cutlass two spoonfuls of vinegar a day.

I'll give Wilby Sicke and Len Ho a cup of seawater a day.

Jim Ladd and Roger Jolly will eat garlic and horseradish bound together with smelly plant glue.

Chivers Metimbers and Downey Hatch will get a daily quart of cider. Our two stowaway female crew members Eve Too and Raisa Anchor will each get two oranges and a lemon a day.

Fourteen days later

Eve and Raisa are cured! I'm brilliant! (Shame about the others, though.) The girls leapt out of their hammocks on the sixth day and raced each other round the ship. They said they hated all that nasty sour fruit but felt much better anyway. They've offered to help me nurse the other ten who are still sick.

1 Poor Walker and Spike are in a bad way. I feel a bit sorry for them. They've still got scurvy and now they've got raging gut ache, too. Must be all that acid.

2 Davy and Andy are in a sour mood. That'll be the vinegar. And they've still got scurvy.

85

3 Poor Wilby and Len keep throwing up. Must be all that seawater. They've still got the scurvy.

4 Everyone steers clear of Jim and Roger. They reek of garlic and they can't stop farting. Ah, now that'll be all the horseradish. No improvement in the scurvy.

5 Chivers and Downey have still got scurvy, but at least they're happy. They keep singing "Roll out the barrel!" and shouting "Cheers!" to all the others. The rest of the crew have all volunteered to try this treatment.

Conclusion

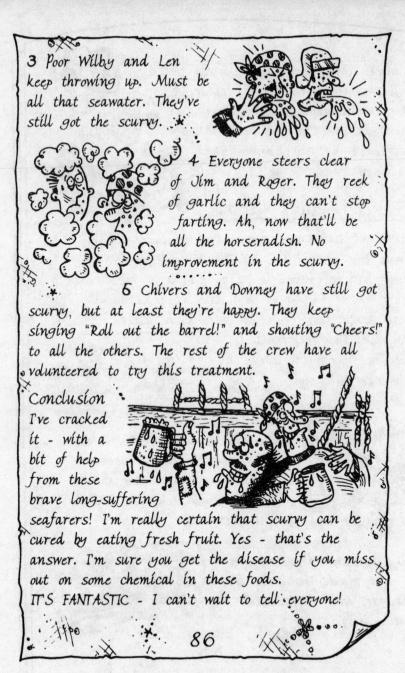

I've cracked it - with a bit of help from these brave long-suffering seafarers! I'm really certain that scurvy can be cured by eating fresh fruit. Yes - that's the answer. I'm sure you get the disease if you miss out on some chemical in these foods.

IT'S FANTASTIC - I can't wait to tell everyone!

James Lind sent his report to Admiral Lord Anson (1697–1762) who was in charge of the Royal Navy. He thought Anson would support him. After all when Anson sailed round the world in 1740–1744 most of his crew had died of scurvy. So what happened next?

a) Lord Anson was impressed. Lind was given a £20,000 reward and in future all seafarers were ordered to eat a lemon a day. No one got scurvy ever again.

b) The Navy ignored Lind's findings and it took another 40 years before they took action.

c) The Navy decided that the acid treatment was better. Lind was sacked from his job as a nuisance and a trouble-maker.

Answer: b) Disgusting but true. The Navy decided that lemons were too expensive. They actually felt it was cheaper to hire new sailors to replace the ones who died. Things only changed after the sailors mutinied and demanded lemons to beat scurvy. Although some sailors didn't like the fruit they changed their minds when lemons and limes were added to their rum ration. But it wasn't until the 1930s that scientists found the mystery chemical that prevented scurvy was ascorbic acid – better known as vitamin C.

A DISGUSTING DIET

So, eat lots of different foods and you'll get everything your body needs to stay healthy. Brilliant! But what happens if you are vegetarian and don't eat meat or fish? Or if you're vegan and don't eat meat, fish or foods made by animals such as milk and eggs? Either way it's fine as long as you get the vitamins and minerals you need.

But eat just a few things and you won't get all the vital goodies. The most disgusting diet of all is not to eat anything. Surprise! Food is good for you, hunger is bad for you. Scientists have found that children who miss breakfast find it hard to learn new things at school. Don't try this excuse. And just look what happens to a really starving body...

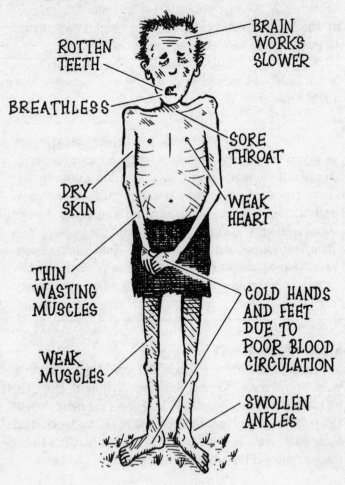

ROTTEN TEETH

BRAIN WORKS SLOWER

BREATHLESS

SORE THROAT

DRY SKIN

WEAK HEART

THIN WASTING MUSCLES

COLD HANDS AND FEET DUE TO POOR BLOOD CIRCULATION

WEAK MUSCLES

SWOLLEN ANKLES

Miserable, isn't it? In the bad old days hunger was a cheap way of punishing naughty children.

Luckily, you're equipped with the perfect gear to chomp any kind of food. The next chapter will really give you something to chew over.

THE MIGHTY MOUTH

Shovel food in your gob and something disgusting happens. Your food, even the stringiest steak and crunchiest carrots, turn into a shredded gooey pulp before vanishing for ever down the black hole of your throat. So what's going on? Get your teeth into these amazing facts.

Dare you discover … what's in your mouth?

Stand in front of mirror. Open wide. Go on – take a look – it won't bite you. What do you see? An amazing chewing machine – that's what.

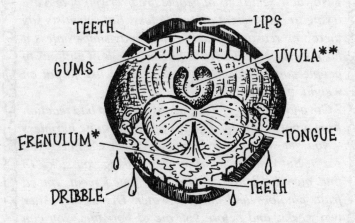

*This supplies your tongue with blood. Can you see the blood vessels? Pretty, aren't they? Well, pretty disgusting really.

**This little dangling bit hangs around in the throat and no one knows quite what it's for. It seems to help you swallow and its name means "little grape" in Latin – can you see why?

THE TALENTED TONGUE

The tongue is a lump of muscle. You can take a good look at it in the mirror, it's one part of your digestive system you can actually see, but don't go showing it to headteachers, parents, etc. Your talented tongue is amazingly agile. It moves around while you eat, talk or even eat and talk at the same time.

Disgusting digestion fact file

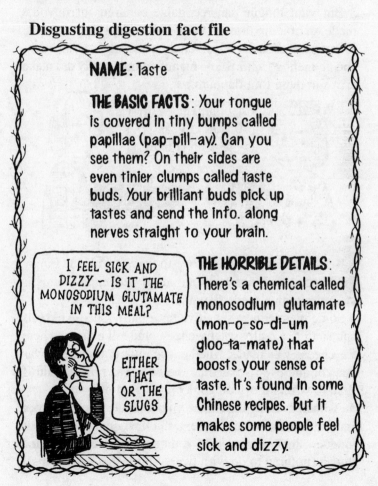

NAME: Taste

THE BASIC FACTS: Your tongue is covered in tiny bumps called papillae (pap-pill-ay). Can you see them? On their sides are even tinier clumps called taste buds. Your brilliant buds pick up tastes and send the info. along nerves straight to your brain.

I FEEL SICK AND DIZZY – IS IT THE MONOSODIUM GLUTAMATE IN THIS MEAL?

EITHER THAT OR THE SLUGS

THE HORRIBLE DETAILS: There's a chemical called monosodium glutamate (mon-o-so-di-um gloo-ta-mate) that boosts your sense of taste. It's found in some Chinese recipes. But it makes some people feel sick and dizzy.

SOME TASTELESS FACTS

1 In traditional Chinese medicine there were five tastes – bitter, salty, sweet, sour and spicy.

2 Modern scientists more or less agree. They say you can detect five tastes – sweet, sour, salty, bitter and umami. This is a sort of meaty, savoury sensation – just think of burgers, yum!

3 But your tongue can recognize hundreds of flavours made up of a mixture of tastes. Take crisps, for example. There are over 70 flavours including chocolate, strawberry, and hedgehog*. (It's true – manufacturers really did make crisps in these foul flavours.)

ER, WEASEL AND ONION. OR IS IT TOAD AND VINEGAR?

* Before you get on the phone to the World Wide Fund for Nature, they don't use any dead hedgehogs – this is an entirely man-made flavour.

4 Some people have sensitive taste buds. Cheese experts can sample a really smelly cheese and tell exactly where the cheese was made, whether the milk that made it was heated, and even what time the cow was milked. But if they're wrong they can get a bit cheesed off.

5 A doctor always looks at your tongue to check your state of health. For example, a thick white scum on your tongue might be caused by a disgusting infection called thrush (nothing to do with tweety-birds that eat worms).

6 In ancient China doctors peered at tongues too. They believed that the appearance of the tongue reflected the health of the rest of the body. Here are a few things they looked for…

a) Whitish tongue = lack of energy.

b) Bright red tongue = body is too hot.

c) Purple/blue tongue or purple spots = blood not moving fast enough.

d) Fur-like growth* on the tongue = death will follow within a week.

*This could really be a sign the body is unwell. The "fur" may be a type of fungus which flourishes when the body's defences, the white blood cells, are weakened by other diseases.

Here are two experiments that are in the best possible taste.

Dare you discover 1… Test your taste

You will need:
2 small cubes of uncooked potato
2 small cubes of apple

What you do:
1 Close your eyes and hold your nose. Ask someone to hand you one of the foods.

2 Put the food in your mouth and try to guess what you're eating. Now try the other food.

3 Stop holding your nose and repeat step 2. What do you notice?

a) It's easier to make out tastes when you hold your nose.

b) It's harder to make out tastes when you hold your nose.

c) Foods taste sweeter when you hold your nose.

Dare you discover 2... Can you change your sense of taste?

You will need:
Your favourite wine gums or fruit-flavoured sweets. (Tell your parents you need them for science homework – if they believe that, you might as well go for extra pocket money while you're at it.)
2 extra extra strong mints or an ice cube. Put it in a glass of water for a few seconds first.

Don't put an ice cube straight from the freezer into your mouth. The freezing cold ice cube might actually freeze the outside of your tongue and make it sore.

What you do:
1 Pop the extra strong mints OR the ice cube in your mouth. Keep it there until it melts.
2 Pop the wine gum in your mouth. What do you notice?
a) You can't taste it easily.
b) It tastes twice as fruity.
c) When you take it out of your mouth it's gone black.

Answers: 1 b) Your sense of smell is stronger than your sense of taste. When you think you're tasting your favourite food – you're really sniffing it. And that's why food tastes like cardboard when you have a real stonker of a cold. 2 a) The ice numbs the tongue so it can't taste so well. The strong taste of the mint blocks out new taste signals from your tongue to your brain for a while. So the news about the taste of the sweet doesn't get through. And after that there's nothing for it. You'll have to brush all traces of the sweet off your teeth.

Disgusting digestion fact file

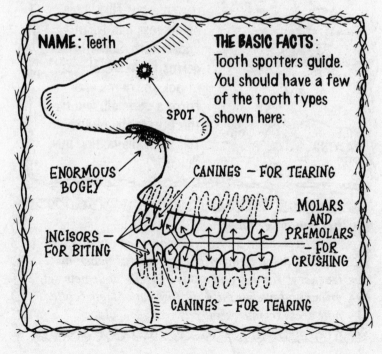

NAME: Teeth

THE BASIC FACTS: Tooth spotters guide. You should have a few of the tooth types shown here:

SPOT

ENORMOUS BOGEY

CANINES – FOR TEARING

INCISORS – FOR BITING

MOLARS AND PREMOLARS – FOR CRUSHING

CANINES – FOR TEARING

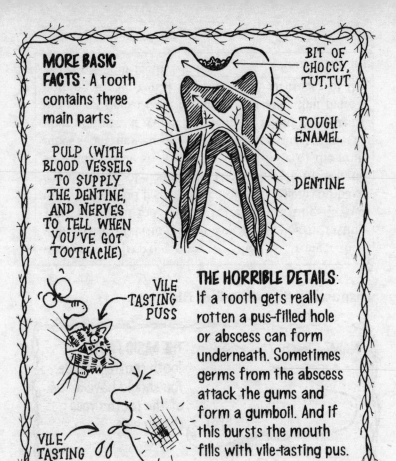

MORE BASIC FACTS: A tooth contains three main parts:

PULP (WITH BLOOD VESSELS TO SUPPLY THE DENTINE, AND NERVES TO TELL WHEN YOU'VE GOT TOOTHACHE)

BIT OF CHOCCY, TUT,TUT

TOUGH ENAMEL

DENTINE

VILE TASTING PUSS

VILE TASTING PUS

THE HORRIBLE DETAILS: If a tooth gets really rotten a pus-filled hole or abscess can form underneath. Sometimes germs from the abscess attack the gums and form a gumboil. And if this bursts the mouth fills with vile-tasting pus. Yeuch!

Bet you never knew!
Your teeth have a crushing power of about 73 kg – that's the weight of one of your slimmer male teachers! You have two sets of teeth. Your new set grows and pushes out your first set of teeth (called milk teeth or baby teeth) as you grow older.

But that's nothing…

• Elephants have 24 molar teeth and they're replaced six times. When the last set of teeth falls out the elephant starves.

POOR OLD THING! IT'LL BE PORRIDGE FROM NOW ON

• Crocodiles grow new teeth whenever they need them. This could be handy for humans, too. You could grow extra teeth to handle all those rubbery school dinners.

I'VE GROWN MINE TO HANDLE RUBBERY SCHOOL CHILDREN

• Some sharks' teeth get replaced every eight days – that's 30,000 teeth in a shark lifetime.

SO WHAT?

B-B-BUT YOU MIGHT LOSE SOME TEETH IF YOU BITE INTO MY RUBBER SUIT…

DREADFUL DENTURES

Humans only get two sets of teeth and when these fall out we're stuck. That's why millions of people have to wear false teeth or dentures. Nowadays these are made from a tough plastic but before then people had to make do with some really disgusting dentures. Here are a few examples...

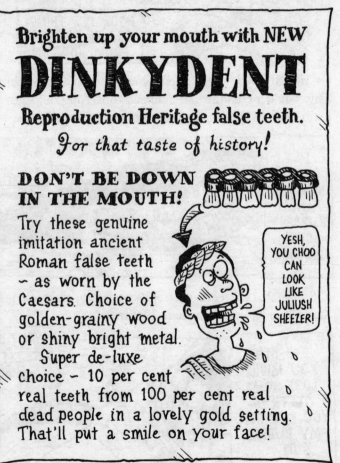

Brighten up your mouth with NEW

DINKYDENT

Reproduction Heritage false teeth.

For that taste of history!

DON'T BE DOWN IN THE MOUTH!

Try these genuine imitation ancient Roman false teeth – as worn by the Caesars. Choice of golden-grainy wood or shiny bright metal.

Super de-luxe choice – 10 per cent real teeth from 100 per cent real dead people in a lovely gold setting. That'll put a smile on your face!

YESH, YOU CHOO CAN LOOK LIKE JULIUSH SHEEZER!

Of course, you'd probably rather not have false teeth. So it's a good idea to take care of the ones you've got.

DISGUSTING EXPRESSIONS

Isn't this an ornamental sign found in public buildings?

Answer: No, this kind of plaque is a disgusting layer of germs and bits of food that builds up around the teeth.

Within three minutes of sucking a sweet the germs lurking in the plaque start making acid to dissolve your teeth. If they make a hole they can cause horrible toothache.

Here are some disgusting ideas to help for making a clean sweep of the problem.

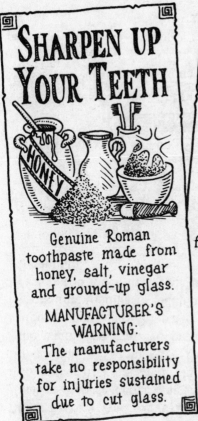

SHARPEN UP YOUR TEETH

Genuine Roman toothpaste made from honey, salt, vinegar and ground-up glass.

MANUFACTURER'S WARNING:
The manufacturers take no responsibility for injuries sustained due to cut glass.

A toothy red letter ~ day ~

Tasteful Victorian toothpaste. Original and unique recipe including ground-up coral and cuttlefish, burnt eggshells, bits of china and cochineal (made from powdered insects). Guaranteed to turn your teeth a pleasing purple colour.

And here are some more sensible ideas.

• Flossing teeth cleans out germs lurking between teeth and near gums – some of their favourite hiding places.

• Chewing a sugar-free chewing gum makes you produce spit. Spit contains chemicals that help combat the acid made by tooth germs, and so helps to keep your teeth clean.

But don't do either of these in science lessons. Instead, you could try this…

TEACHER'S TOOTH TEST

Does your teacher know the tooth – er, sorry, the truth about teeth? Find out now as you ask...

1 How many teeth does a child of ten have?

a) About 52

b) About 12

c) About 26

2 Which of the following isn't a raw material of modern toothpastes?

a) Chalk

b) Seaweed

c) Washing-up liquid

Answers: 1 a) With a bit of luck your teacher will fall for this one. Although they're not all on display, a child of ten should have grown-up teeth hidden under their first set. And when you take a bite the vibration makes all these teeth twang slightly like guitar strings. **2** Another trick question. They're *all* used. The chalk is ground up to make a fine powder that cleans the teeth. The seaweed provides a chemical called alginate that binds the paste together. The detergent gives the toothpaste bubbles and makes cleaning easier. Too much detergent and you'd be foaming at the mouth.

SUPER-SLURPING SPIT

Picture your favourite food. A giant pizza with your favourite topping and hot bubbling cheese. Sizzling juicy burgers or crispy fried chicken and a giant pile of fries. Can't you smell that lovely just-cooked aroma? Are you drooling yet? You should be. Just thinking about food makes your mouth water – and the smell and sight of food helps even more. Your spit is ready and waiting to come out whenever you need it.

Spit is made by six salivary glands – two under your tongue, two under your jaw and two under your ears. When you get mumps the salivary glands under your ear get infected by a virus and swell up so your face looks fat. But cheer up face-ache – help is at hand...

Ye Olde Mumps Cure

1 Take a donkey's lead and put it around the patient's neck.

2 Lead them three times round a pig sty.

After that embarrassing experience you probably wouldn't care about having a swollen face. Every day your sensational salivary glands squirt out 1–1.5 litres of spit. All of this you swallow. Some people spit it out instead – disgusting! Don't do it. It's a waste of good spit – look what it can do for you.

Have you ever eaten really dry food, like bread, when your mouth is also dry and there's nothing to drink? Disgusting, isn't it? By making your food wet, spit makes it easier to swallow. And spit helps you taste food. You can only taste food by detecting chemicals floating around in water. When food is dry its chemicals can't flow amongst the taste-buds so it seems tasteless.

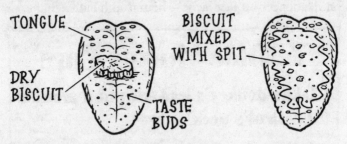

TONGUE

BISCUIT MIXED WITH SPIT

DRY BISCUIT

TASTE BUDS

Spit has some disgusting ingredients, such as mucus – basically the same stuff that streams from your nose when you have a cold. This makes it quite slimy and stringy so you can suck it back into your mouth. There's no need to demonstrate this interesting scientific accomplishment just now.

I SAID, THERE'S NO NEED TO DEMONSTRATE THIS INTERESTING SCIENTIFIC ACCOMPLISHMENT JUST NOW!!

Then there are the germs. Your spit is swarming with them. In fact, there could be 15,000,000,000 (15 billion) bacteria in your mouth at any one time. Many germs end up getting eaten when you swallow spit. Hmm, tasty! But strangely enough, spit contains chemicals that kill some germs, and dentists have found that spit helps to keep your mouth clean and free from infection.

Spit also contains a waste product called urea that your body makes from spare protein. And guess what? You'll find it in urine too – it gives urine its yellow colour. If you eat too much protein your body makes more urea and your spit also turns yellow. Either that or you've been slurping extra thick banana milkshakes. But the real magic spit ingredient is an enzyme called amylase (am-me-laze) that helps to rip carbohydrates into the sugars that make them up. (You can find out more about enzymes on page 127.)

DISGUSTING EATING HABITS
Mealtimes used to be tough for kids.

One of the worst things to do when you're eating is to eat too quickly. Like these people…

FAST FOOD FACTS

• Do you like pickled onions? If you find them disgusting you'll be horrified to hear that Pat Donahue crunched 91 in 68 seconds in Victoria, Canada in 1978.

• Peter Dowdeswell ate 144 prunes in 31.27 seconds in Rochester, New York, in 1986. Prunes are full of fibre and are well known for making you want to go to the toilet. So you can guess what the next world record was…

AH YES, CERTAINLY SIR. YOU'LL FIND THEM OVER BY THE…

• In the same year Peter also ate 91.44 metres of spaghetti in 12 seconds in Halesowen, Britain.
And then … well you can guess what happened next.

DISGUSTING DIGESTION EXPRESSIONS

GLASS OF LEMONADE?

NO, THANK YOU, IT CAUSES ERUCTATION

Is this dangerous?

BIGGER, BETTER BURPS

Huge hearty great burps are just your body's way of getting rid of some of the air you swallowed with your food. The faster you eat and the more you talk as you eat the more you burp. It's easier to burp when you're standing up. So imagine a posh party where people are eating and talking, and drinking fizzy drinks (with lots of gas) and standing up, too. They all want to burp but they're far too polite.

By the way, if you ever go to lunch in Arabia it's OK to burp loudly after the meal. It's considered a sign of good manners. This is sensible because you've got to let the air out somehow.

CONGRATULATIONS! You've managed to eat your supper without hiccups, heartburn, burping or food dribbling out of your nostrils. NOW for the tricky bit. Can you keep it down?

THE STAGGERING STOMACH

You're in control. You decide what you eat, don't you? Think again. There's a part of your body that seems to have a mind of its own. It's a muscular bag just under the left part of your chest. It makes you feel sick, it makes you feel queasy and it rumbles. And it does a whole load of other tricks, too … it's staggering!

Disgusting digestion fact file

NAME: Stomach

THE BASIC FACTS: The stomach is a storage tank for your food. Its job is to mix and squash food to make it easier to digest. The stomach also makes enzymes that help to digest protein. And it does all this while you get on with your life.

THE HORRIBLE DETAILS: The stomach is staggeringly horrible. For example, there's a type of germ that lives quite happily in the stomach eating up your half-digested food.

GOOD OLD STOMACH!

RUMBLE, CHURN, GURGLE, PLOP!

STAGGERING STOMACH STATISTICS
The human stomach can hold up to 1.5 litres of food.
   Mind you, that's nothing.
• It takes your speedy stomach just 60 minutes to digest a cup of tea and a jam sandwich.

• Milk, eggs and meat take a bit longer. Eat a boiled egg with a ham sandwich washed down with a milk-shake and it'll take 3–4 hours to clear your stomach.

• But if you really want your stomach to work harder try a huge three-course dinner with soup and meat, and fruit for afters. That'll take your tired-out tum 6–7 hours to process.

HURRY UP, STOMACH

I'M GOING AS FAST AS I CAN

• A wolf's stomach can hold 4.5 litres of food. Does that mean they have to "wolf" their meals?

• Cow stomachs can hold 182 litres of food – that's enough to fill a bath if the cow sicked it up again. (Cows have an advantage – they actually have four stomachs not one.) One stomach is used for storing the grass before they sick it up and re-chew it – lovely! This is known as "chewing the cud" – or rumination (roo-min-ay-shun) as the scientists call it. The other stomachs are useful for storing the re-chewed grass whilst it rots. (Rotten grass is easier to digest.) Yum-yum!

GRASS IN

GRASS OUT (COWPAT)

• The mangrove monkey eats leaves all day. It needs an extra-big tum to hold all those leaves and its stomach weighs as much as the rest of its body. If you had a stomach this big you really would be staggering.

STAGGERING STOMACH QUIZ

How well do you know your own stomach?

1 The word stomach comes from the Greek word for "throat". TRUE/FALSE

2 Butterflies in your stomach aren't anything to do with the stomach. TRUE/FALSE

3 It's possible to live without a stomach. TRUE/FALSE

4 It's possible to eat and eat until your stomach bursts. TRUE/FALSE

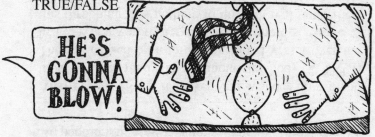

5 When you eat ice cream the cold freezes your stomach. TRUE/FALSE

6 Your stomach stops moving when you're asleep. TRUE/FALSE

7 Your stomach produces an acid strong enough to dissolve a lump of bone. TRUE/FALSE

Answers: 1 TRUE It makes you wonder how much those Greeks really knew about the body. 2 TRUE They're caused by a throbbing blood vessel over the heart. When you're nervous you're more sensitive to this throbbing. It's nothing to do with real butterflies. 3 TRUE Some people do. You just need to eat regular small meals instead of three big meals. 4 FALSE Don't worry this is impossible. If your stomach gets really full the opening at its base simply widens to let more food into your guts. But that's not an excuse to go and pig out. 5 TRUE That's "freeze" in the sense of stopping it moving, not turning it to ice. The cold stops your stomach churning for up to half an hour. 6 FALSE The stomach carries on churning slowly even while you're dreaming. In fact, if you dream you're eating, your stomach thinks the dream is real and makes extra digestive juices. 7 TRUE The stomach wall contains 3.5 million pits that make 0.5 per cent hydrochloric (hi-dro-cloor-rick) acid. This is strong enough to dissolve a lump of food in a few hours. A boa constrictor's stomach juices can even turn a whole pig into goo. Yuck! A more concentrated form of the acid is used in industry to dissolve out zinc from scrap iron (don't try this at home).

The vital goings on in the stomach were first probed by a scientist with a taste for staggeringly sick experiments.

Hall of fame: Lazzaro Spallanzani (1729–1799)
Nationality: Italian
Brainy Laz wanted to be a lawyer until his even brainier cousin Laura Bassi (1711–1778) talked him into

becoming a scientist. As luck would have it, Laura happened to be the world's first woman professor of physics and introduced Laz to her scientist pals. So Laz became interested in many areas of science including such scintillating topics as where thunder clouds and sponges come from. (That's the sea creatures, not the cake you eat for tea or the thing you use in the bath.)

Laz had a hands-on approach to science. When locals claimed that Lake Ventasso in Italy had a giant whirlpool, the brave scientist built a raft and sailed across the lake – so proving the whirlpool didn't exist. In 1788 he decided to study volcanoes so he climbed a series of Italian craters. At Mount Etna in Sicily he had to be rescued after getting knocked out by poisonous gases. Undaunted he climbed Mount Vulcano but gave up when his walking stick caught fire and his feet got burnt.

Finally, by watching Mount Stromboli he discovered that gas explosions are the reason rocks fly out of volcanoes.

It took more than a few disgusting sights to stop Laz in his tracks. In 1765 he became interested in how some animals can re-grow parts of their bodies. So he cut up thousands of unfortunate worms, slugs and salamanders.

(He discovered that younger animals are best at re-growing.) He took the same fearless approach to his work on digestion. Would you want to make yourself sick? Laz did – in the interests of science – umpteen times.

Then he studied vile vomit. Amongst other disgusting discoveries he found that stomach acid could dissolve soft bone and gristle but this took longer than ordinary meat.

DISGUSTING DIGESTION EXPRESSIONS

One doctor says to another:

I MAY BE ABOUT TO REGURGITATE

Should you take cover?

Answer: YES. It's the posh word for being sick.

This can be triggered by:

a) Fear – e.g. a science test.

b) A horrible sight or smell – e.g. a revolting science experiment.

c) Disgusting food or poison or germs – e.g. a school dinner.

Oddly enough, doctors also use the term to describe leaking of the blood from a dodgy valve in the heart.

A SICKENING STORY

You're dizzy, you turn pale, you sweat and your mouth is full of spit. You're about to chuck up. Run for the bathroom! The muscles in your lower body and stomach all squeeze together until your half-digested food erupts from your gullet. Vomiting, as it's called, is controlled by a part of your brain known as the vomiting centre. It's well-known that throwing up can be triggered by fear. Scientists don't quite know how this happens. They think that your nerves produce chemicals that make your stomach heave when you're scared of something.

What your vomit looks like depends on how long it's been in your stomach. If it's only been there for a few seconds it won't look too different from when you ate it. Especially if it happens to be carrot stew. But if it's been down for a couple of hours it will be a thick soupy mess. Scientists call this disgusting substance chyme (pronounced chime). How chyming, er, sorry, charming.

COULD YOU BE A SCIENTIST?

Have you ever bent over and thought you were about to be sick? Don't try to do it now – take my word for it, it happens. The half-digested food slips out of your stomach. The acid mixture can burn the oesophagus so badly that some sufferers think they're having a heart attack. This is called heartburn. Some scientists looked at the effects of exercise on heartburn. They measured the amount of acid stomach juice there was in the oesophagus one hour after...

a) Running
b) Weightlifting
c) Cycling

Which do you think caused the most heartburn?

UNBEARABLE ULCERS

Life can be tough for the stomach, too. One of the nastiest things that can happen to a stomach is when it starts digesting itself! This is what's known as an ulcer. Ulcers can be unbearably painful and need to be treated with substances such as chalk (yes, chalk) that neutralize the acid.

Your stomach has three lines of defence.

1 A thick layer of jelly-like mucus (the same stuff as slimy, runny snot, remember). This stops the acid leaking out and causing an ulcer.

2 A wall of 800 million cells wedged together to block

any acid that does escape. The cells are being replaced and every three days you get a brand new shiny pink stomach lining!

3 If the stomach gets too acidic the cells make a chemical called bicarbonate of soda. This is actually the same chemical you find in alka-seltzer and other medicines that settle an upset tum. The chemical neutralizes the acid so it isn't so strong.

Normally, though, ulcers only happen to stressed-out grown-ups.

HOW ARE YOU GETTING ON WITH YEAR 5, MR SIMPKINS?

Scientists reckon that ulcers are caused by bacteria that stop the stomach lining from making so much lovely protective mucus. This allows the stomach's acid to make a hole in the lining – and that's the ulcer. Sounds painful.

Talking about the guts, which we were a moment ago, it's time to leave the stomach and check out the intestines. And the going is going to get seriously disgusting from now on.

POO-EY PONG

DISGUSTING GUT FEELINGS

Welcome to the intestines – the most horrible bit of your digestive system. The place where it's all happening. It's where fats, carbohydrates and proteins get broken down to smaller chemicals and sucked into the blood. And it's home to all sorts of disgusting goings-on.

Remember Gutzache's epic journey through the guts? Here's the map he used. It'll help you find your way around this chapter, too.

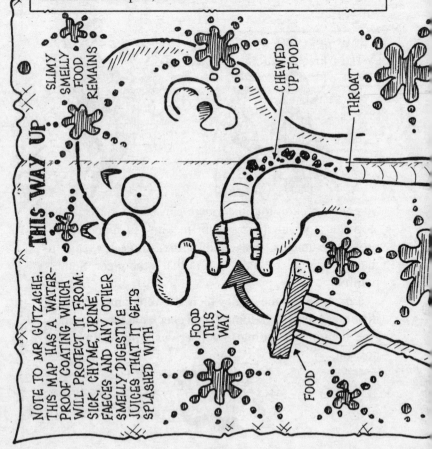

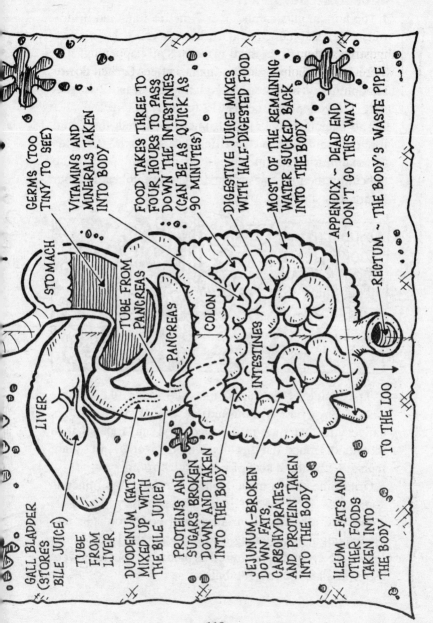

GERMS (TOO TINY TO SEE)

VITAMINS AND MINERALS TAKEN INTO BODY

FOOD TAKES THREE TO FOUR HOURS TO PASS DOWN THE INTESTINES (CAN BE AS QUICK AS 90 MINUTES)

DIGESTIVE JUICE MIXES WITH HALF-DIGESTED FOOD

MOST OF THE REMAINING WATER SUCKED BACK INTO THE BODY

APPENDIX ~ DEAD END ~ DON'T GO THIS WAY

RECTUM ~ THE BODY'S WASTE PIPE

STOMACH

TUBE FROM PANCREAS

PANCREAS

COLON

INTESTINES

LIVER

TUBE FROM LIVER

GALL BLADDER (STORES BILE JUICE)

DUODENUM (FATS MIXED UP WITH THE BILE JUICE)

PROTEINS AND SUGARS BROKEN DOWN AND TAKEN INTO THE BODY

JEJUNUM~BROKEN DOWN FATS, CARBOHYDRATES AND PROTEIN TAKEN INTO THE BODY

ILEUM ~ FATS AND OTHER FOODS TAKEN INTO THE BODY

TO THE LOO

119

GRUESOME GUTS FACTS

1 The human guts can be over 7 metres long and if they weren't tightly coiled and curled up you'd have to be 9 metres tall to fit them all in.

2 The duodenum got its name after Greek doctor Herophilus (4th century BC) claimed it was 12 fingers long. ("Duodenum" means "12 fingers" in Greek.)

3 The ancient Greeks and Romans believed you could foretell the future by sacrificing a sheep to the gods and peering at its intestines. On the whole, the more unhealthy the intestines looked, the more unhealthy your future was supposed to be.

4 The inside of the small intestine looks like a furry carpet. The "fur" is thousands of tiny sticking out bits called villi that suck in digested food and transfer it to the blood. Ironed flat this area would cover 20–40 square metres – about the size of a large classroom.

5 Gruesome stones made from waste food and minerals sometimes form in the guts. These bezoar (be-zo-ar) stones are also found in sheep and goat stomachs and were thought to have magical powers. In the 17th century they were ground up and used as medicines but they were as useless as a square football.

6 In fifth-century India doctors were not afraid to perform operations to remove blockages in the guts. They cut open the patient and afterwards joined the sides of the cut using … ants. Yes, ants. They got a giant black ant to bite the sides of the wound then cut the ant's head off. This left the jaws in position just like a little stitch. Luckily your guts can't feel pain apart from a bit of cramp. So at least the operation didn't hurt the human patient, even if the ants were a bit cut up about it.

Dare you discover … what bile juice does to fats?

You will need:
Washing-up liquid
A bowl of warm water
Cooking oil

What you do:
1 Pour a little cooking oil into the water. The oil will float on the water. This is like the fat in your intestines.
2 Add a drop of the washing-up liquid representing the bile juice. Give the mixture a rapid stir.
What happens next?
a) The oil sinks to the bottom of the bowl and forms a kind of sludge.

b) The oil, washing-up liquid and water mix together in lots of little bubbles.

c) The oil, washing-up liquid and water form huge bubbles that don't burst easily.

GRUESOME GREETINGS

You might wonder how all this activity is controlled by your body. Why doesn't the food in one part of the intestine simply stop moving so that the rest of your supper piles up behind it?

In fact, special chemicals in the blood called hormones carry messages from one part of the body to another to control this vital job. Just imagine if you could hear these messages – what would they say?

One hormone is called secretin (see-creet-in) and here's its message...

Another hormone is called cholecystokinin (kole-sis-toe-ki-nin) – we'll let it speak for itself.

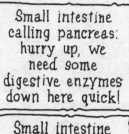

Small intestine calling pancreas: hurry up, we need some digestive enzymes down here quick!

Small intestine calling body: you're not as hungry as you think you are – lay off that cream cake!

Small intestine calling gall bladder: where's that bile juice you promised us? We need a big squirt now!

Meanwhile, the guts also keep in touch using nerves like a kind of telephone line. Let's listen in to a few more conversations

Small intestine to brain control centre: everything's under control. Things are moving nicely. No, hold on – looks like we've got a problem. It's an alien substance – could be a school dinner. Tell the vomiting centre it's action stations. Get ready to heave!

THE GRUMBLING APPENDIX

Sometimes when the appendix gets infected by germs it swells up like a disgusting pus-filled balloon. It can even explode.

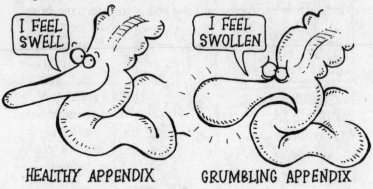

HEALTHY APPENDIX   GRUMBLING APPENDIX

This appalling ailment is called appendicitis and in serious cases the appendix has to be removed. But if the infection isn't too bad the body's white cells guzzle most of the germs and the appendix gets better. If the germs multiply again you get more pain. This delightful condition is known as a "grumbling appendix". No doubt it makes the patients grumble too. But it could be worse. It could be a dodgy colon.

CUT OUT THE COLON

The colon is 1.5 metres long. It's the last bit of the intestines and the name given to the : sign in punctuation. So don't be surprised if your teacher finds a "colon" in a library book. The colon stores your poo before it's pushed out of your body. During this time the walls of the colon suck much of the remaining water from the poo. This stops you spending your life on the toilet getting rid of watery diarrhoea.

Top surgeon Sir William Arbuthnot Lane (1856–1943) was keen on ballroom dancing and designing new types of surgical instruments. But he wasn't too keen on colons. He thought they were useless and caused disease when germs escaped from the colon to infect the body. And he claimed the victim smelt of graveyards. Willie also said people with dodgy colons had cold, bluish ears, cold noses, clammy sweaty hands and...

An appearance of age, distress and disappointment which is most pathetic, particularly in the young

LOOKS AREN'T EVERYTHING

Well, Willie was in the know when it came to colons. His claim to fame was to discover the sudden twists and turns in the colon now known as Lane's kinks.

Worried about the appearance of his patients, Willie invented an operation in which the offending colon was removed. This was fine, so long as the victim, sorry patient, didn't mind the consequences. These involved spending the rest of their life with a hole in their guts through which their poo passed into a bag. Yuck! Fortunately, other doctors criticised Lane for performing the operation unnecessarily. And so Lane's treatment of the colon came to a : er, sorry, a full stop.

Meanwhile, back in the intestines things are really hotting up. Boiling and bubbling as mysterious chemicals get to work. Enter the energetic enzymes. Is your gut getting fizz-ical? Better find out now...

AM I TOO LATE FOR THE NEXT CHAPTER?

NO, YOU'RE JUST EN-ZYME!

ENERGETIC ENZYMES

Look inside your body and you'll see a gruesome assembly of bones, muscles and blood. But look closer and you'll see a fizzing mass of chemical reactions that would make most chemists green with envy. It's all done with enzymes. Without them digestion would be a dead loss and so would you. But with them you're fizzing with physical fitness. So what do enzymes do all day?

Disgusting digestion fact file

NAME: Enzymes

THE BASIC FACTS: 1 An enzyme is a protein that changes other chemicals. In digestion, enzymes help to break other chemicals to pieces.

2 Every cell in your body contains over 3,000 different enzymes.

THE HORRIBLE DETAILS: If you didn't have enzymes the only other way to digest your food would be to heat your body. This also breaks the food chemicals up. Unfortunately, your body would need to be 300°C (572°F) to do this. So you'd need to cook yourself to enjoy your food.

Dare you discover ... how enzymes work?

You will need:

A hardboiled egg. (Ask an adult to boil the egg for six minutes.) Cool the egg and peel off the shell.

Biological washing powder

A jar and spoon

What you do:

1 Add eight tablespoonfuls of warm water to the jar.

2 Ask your adult helper to put on protective gloves and mix in one tablespoonful of washing powder. They should stir the mixture until the powder disappears.

3 Add a piece of boiled egg white (not the yellow yolk).

4 Wrap the jar in a towel and leave in a warm place such as an airing cupboard for two days.

5 Take a look at the piece of egg white. What do you notice?

a) The egg is a horrible brown colour.

b) The egg has turned into a white liquid.

c) The egg has got smaller.

Answer: c) The washing powder contains enzymes that break down the protein in the egg into smaller chemicals that dissolve in the water. This is exactly what happens in your guts.

Bet you never knew!
Enzymes make heat as they rip chemicals to pieces inside your guts. That's why Arctic sledge drivers give their dogs butter to eat in very cold weather. Butter is digested by enzymes and this makes enough heat to warm the dogs. And if enzymes make heat, let's visit a few hot spots.

Disgusting digestion fact file

NAME: Pancreas

THE BASIC FACTS:
The pancreas is like a chemical factory pumping out enzymes to digest carbohydrates, fat and protein. It makes 1.5 litres of digestive juice a day.

ENZYMES ← PANCREAS

HORMONES

INSULIN   GLYCOGEN

THE HORRIBLE DETAILS: The pancreas also makes two hormones – insulin and glycogen that control the sugar that gets to your muscles to provide energy. Lack of insulin causes a horrible disease called diabetes.

A WORTHY WINNER?

Scientists toil away for years until at last they make a great discovery. But who should get the glory for discoveries? Take insulin, for example. When scientists found out about insulin they were able to give extra insulin to people with diabetes. Thousands of lives were saved. In Sweden a committee met to award the 1923 Nobel Prize for Medicine… But who should get credit? These were the main contenders:

Frederick Banting (1891–1941)

A First World War hero. Like many scientists of his time, Banting was convinced there was something in the pancreas that prevented diabetes. He discovered insulin in 1922.

Charles Best (1899–1978)

Brilliant laboratory assistant who helped make Banting's work possible. He and Banting bravely injected one another with insulin to make sure it was safe.

James Collip (1892–1965)

A talented chemist. Showed Banting and Best how to make a pure kind of insulin suitable for injecting into humans.

John Macleod (1876–1935)
In charge of the lab in Canada where Banting and Best worked. Didn't think much of Banting as a scientist. Was on holiday when insulin was discovered.

Two scientists were awarded the coveted Nobel Prize in 1923 – but which two?

Disgusting digestion fact file

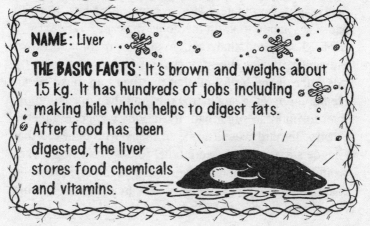

NAME: Liver

THE BASIC FACTS: It's brown and weighs about 1.5 kg. It has hundreds of jobs including making bile which helps to digest fats. After food has been digested, the liver stores food chemicals and vitamins.

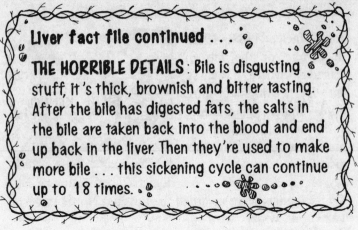

Liver fact file continued . . .

THE HORRIBLE DETAILS: Bile is disgusting stuff, it's thick, brownish and bitter tasting. After the bile has digested fats, the salts in the bile are taken back into the blood and end up back in the liver. Then they're used to make more bile . . . this sickening cycle can continue up to 18 times.

One man played a vital role in probing the liver's secrets…

Hall of fame: Claude Bernard (1813–1878)
Nationality: French

Bernard was the son of a humble grape picker but when he died he was the first French scientist to enjoy a full state funeral. Well, maybe "enjoy" isn't the right word since he was dead at the time. Young Claude Bernard didn't want to be a scientist. He wanted to be a playwright. Fortunately (for science), his plays were so bad that Claude took up medicine instead.

He discovered that carbohydrates are broken down into sugars during digestion and fats are broken down by bile juice. Then he found that the liver can make sugar. He fed a dog on a sugar-free diet and then opened up its liver to find that sugar had mysteriously appeared there.

Mrs Bernard was just one of many who believed that Claude's experiments were cruel to dogs. No dog owner would allow Claude near their pets and the scientist soon found that his programme of research was in trouble owing to a shortage of subjects.

So he took to kidnapping dogs for his research. One day one of Bernard's stolen dogs escaped from the lab and ran home to its owner. Unfortunately, the owner happened to be the Chief of Police and he came round to ask the scientist some awkward questions…

What do you think happened next?

a) Claude Bernard was sentenced to three years' hard labour for cruelty to dogs. Mrs Bernard was the chief prosecution witness.

b) The scientist was let off after paying a hefty fine and making a big donation to the local stray dogs home.

c) Bernard made a grovelling apology and was let off with a caution.

Answer: c) And you'll be pleased to know the dog lived happily ever after with his owner.

DISGUSTING LIVER DISEASES

The ancient peoples of Babylonia (modern Iraq) had a disgusting method of finding out what liver disease a person was suffering from. Let's take a look at this ancient tablet. (That's a clay tablet, not the sort of tablet you'd take for an upset tum or sore throat.)

AN ANCIENT
TABLET

How to spot liver disease
You need one sheep
1. Blow into the sheep's nostrils
2. Sacrifice the sheep to the gods and look at its liver
3. Compare the liver to a clay model. If there's anything different about the real animal liver you'll have this problem, too.

AN ANCIENT
TABLET

Stones similar to those in the guts can also appear in the liver. They often form in the gall bladder where they do no harm unless they get big enough to stop bile from reaching the guts. If there is a blockage, the bile leaks into the blood and ends up in the skin and eyeballs. Bile contains colours made from waste chemicals from the liver and these turn the skin and eyeballs a tasteful yellow. This disgusting condition is known as jaundice.

CAN YOU TELL WHICH OF THESE YELLOW OBJECTS HAS JAUNDICE?

Nowadays, it's easy for surgeons to crush the stones or in the worst cases simply whip out the gall bladder in one easy operation. Meanwhile, your body is busy using up all your hard-digested food.

JUICY JOULES

Your blood carries the juicy digested food chemicals to all parts of your body. In your muscles the chemicals are ripped apart to produce the energy that keeps you going. We measure this energy in kilojoules (ke-lo-jools) or kJ for short.

Bet you never knew!
A boy aged 9–11 needs 9,500 kJ of food per day to keep going and between the ages of 12 and 14 this goes up to 11,000 kJ. A girl of 9–11 needs only 8,500 kJ per day and at 12–14 she needs 9,000 kJ. So why do girls need less food? Some girls are smaller or less active than boys. Or maybe they're just not so greedy.

Compare that with…
• A canary needs just 46 kJ a day to avoid hopping off its perch for good.
• An elephant uses up a jumbo 385,000 kJ a day.
• A rocket needs 100,000,000 (one hundred million) kJ to get into space.
Confusing isn't it? Maybe this quiz will help you digest the facts.

ENERGY QUIZ

Can you find the food with the right amount of energy to keep you going through each challenge?

CHALLENGE	FOOD
1 Shovelling snow for an hour.	**a)** A glass of milk. 418 kJ 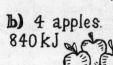
2 Cycling for ten minutes. 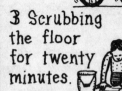	**b)** 4 apples. 840 kJ 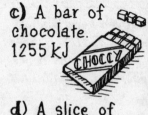
3 Scrubbing the floor for twenty minutes.	**c)** A bar of chocolate. 1255 kJ 
4 Swimming round the pool for four minutes without touching the sides.	**d)** A slice of of buttered toast. 314 kJ
5 Dancing for ten minutes.	**e)** 300 grams (10.6 oz) of sausages. 3000 kJ 

WARNING If you eat too little food you'll feel horribly hungry and weak and light-headed. You might even faint. Eat too much and you'll put on extra fat.

A HOT PROBLEM

Producing all that energy also generates heat. That's why you feel really hot and sweaty after a run. Every day we produce the same heat as burning 500g of coal. Twelve people sitting in a room give off as much heat as a small electric fire. Luckily, the blood takes the heat outwards to the skin where it escapes into the air through the pores in your skin. Phew – that's a relief!

137

Sometimes the heat takes water away from your body in the form of sweat and this also cools you down. But if you've got too much water in your body there's another way to get rid of it. Any idea what that might be?

GOING ROUND THE BEND

You can't get away from the toilet. Ultimately it will command your presence with all the power of a giant magnet. Once your breakfast has worked its way through your system, your body will insist on it. It doesn't matter how busy you are – even if it's the middle of a vital science test. You've gotta do what you've gotta do.

But why? The story starts with a couple of rather crucial organs – the kidneys.

Disgusting digestion fact file

NAME: Kidneys

THE BASIC FACTS: You've got two – one on either side of your body – although you only need one to stay alive. Each one is about 11 x 6cm and its job is to filter spare water and waste chemicals from your blood.

THE HORRIBLE DETAILS: The waste stuff is urine – that's pee to you.

SUPPER'S READY, IT'S YOUR FAVOURITE – STEAK AND KIDNEY PIE

KIDNEYS? ACTUALLY I'M NOT VERY HUNGRY, DAD.

FANTASTIC FILTERS

Every day about 1,700 litres of blood flows through your kidneys. Now, as you may have noticed, you don't have that much blood. So we're talking about the same blood going through the kidneys lots of times.

Here's what happens...

Just imagine your kidneys as a pair of fantastic coffee filters. (They do filter coffee along with everything else.)

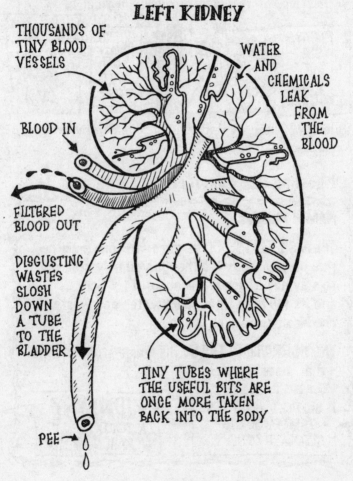

LEFT KIDNEY

THOUSANDS OF TINY BLOOD VESSELS

WATER AND CHEMICALS LEAK FROM THE BLOOD

BLOOD IN

FILTERED BLOOD OUT

DISGUSTING WASTES SLOSH DOWN A TUBE TO THE BLADDER

TINY TUBES WHERE THE USEFUL BITS ARE ONCE MORE TAKEN BACK INTO THE BODY

PEE →

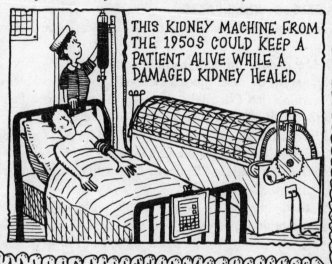

THIS KIDNEY MACHINE FROM THE 1950S COULD KEEP A PATIENT ALIVE WHILE A DAMAGED KIDNEY HEALED

DISGUSTING DIGESTION EXPRESSIONS

COFFEE?

BETTER NOT, I MIGHT HAVE MICTURITION (MICK-TUR-RISH-EON) PROBLEMS

Shouldn't she be in hospital?

USELESS URINE FACTS

Shock the whole school with the extent of your useless knowledge.

1 Most adults produce 1–2 litres of urine a day. That's 40,000 litres in a lifetime, enough to fill 500 baths. (Warning: it's extremely anti-social to pee in one bath, let alone 500.)

2 By the time the bladder has about 0.3 litres it's already feeling full and needs to take a leak.

3 When the bladder fills up, its sides stretch until they're as thin as an onion skin.

4 The opening at the bottom of the bladder is operated by the brain. That's why you don't wet yourself (or at least not very often). Babies don't know how to do this, and that's why they wear nappies. When you go to sleep, messages from your brain keep the opening locked to prevent little disasters in the night.

5 You produce pee faster if you take a deep breath. This allows your diaphragm, the muscle above your liver, to push down on your guts. This in turn squashes the bladder and forces the urine to squirt down its exit tube. Why not try this fascinating experiment for yourself?

6 Urine is about 96 per cent water. The rest is a mix of urea (remember, that's a waste chemical made by your body), and a bit of waste protein and salt. It's a bit smelly but it's usually germ-free…

7 That's why urine was once used to wash wounds on the battlefield. No need to try this next time you get a cut.

8 Most of the time urine is yellow – that's the urea. But sometimes it can be a different colour – such as red, that's when you've eaten too much beetroot. And disgusting facts such as this were once incredibly useful to a breed of...

USELESS URINE DOCTORS

Sometimes your doctor will ask for a sample of your urine. This can help to detect certain diseases. But for hundreds of years doctors thought that you could identify every kind of disease by looking at the patient's urine. Some doctors even tasted it, too. Erk!

In the Middle Ages Spanish urine doctor, Arnold of Villanova, said:

If you find nothing wrong with the patient's urine, but he still insists he has a headache, tell him it is an obstruction of the liver. Continue to speak of obstruction, it is a word he won't understand, but it sounds important.

Surely doctors aren't like that nowadays. They wouldn't use long words just to confuse their patients ... would they?

DISGUSTING EXPRESSIONS

ARE YOU HAVING PROBLEMS WITH YOUR DEFAECATION?

How should she answer? Clue: it's nothing to do with Christmas paper chains, they're *decorations*.

Answer: Defaecation is the posh medical term for making poo. For most people this is once a day or once every two days. But people who eat lots of fibre can defaecate *five times* per day. Bet they get through a fortune in loo rolls.

FOUL FAECES

You remember all that waste food piling up in the colon? Well, it's got to go some time. So every day some of it is shoved out of the anus – usually about 150g for a child. About three-quarters of this is water and the rest is waste food such as fibre and germs. Lovely!

Note: anus = the hole in your bum where the waste products come out. Not to be confused with Uranus which is a distant planet. Clearly you wouldn't want your anus to be that distant.

COULD YOU BE A SCIENTIST?

You are a doctor. Two patients see you. One says...

Doctor, doctor, my poo is red.
1 What do you say?
a) It's blood. You'll be dead in a week.
b) You've got a liver disease that's turned your bile red.
c) Stop eating so many tomatoes.
The other patient says…
Doctor, doctor, my poo is blue!
2 What do you say?
a) You have a rare colon disease.
b) That's impossible – you must be an alien.
c) Stop eating those blue food-colourings!

Answers: 1 c) 2 c)

CRUNCHED-UP CONSTIPATION

When you're very worried you'd think your body would help you feel better. But it doesn't. Instead the vagus nerve for some reason doesn't send the signals from the brain that make you go to the toilet. As a result the poo piles up in the colon where its moisture is sucked back into the blood. The poo becomes dry and crammed together – that's constipation. So it's painful to get rid of – and that really is a worry. And here's another worry – sometimes stress can speed up peristalsis resulting in diarrhoea and extra farts.

If this happens to you, maybe you'd like to try Sir William Arbuthnot Lane's patent constipation remedy…

COD LIVER OIL (MADE FROM DEAD FISH)

CONSTIPATION CURE

OLIVE OIL

LIQUID PARAFFIN (IDEAL FUEL FOR LAMPS)

JUST ONE TEASPOON WILL KEEP YOU GOING ALL DAY!

The paraffin acts like oil in a rusty bike chain. It gets the poo moving again. No, on second thoughts better not – you wouldn't want your guts to turn into a paraffin lamp would you now? And there are enough dangerous gases down there already.

DISGUSTING DIGESTION EXPRESSIONS

YOU'VE GOT A FLATULENCE PROBLEM

Does this need surgery?

Answer: No, just a clothes peg over the nose. Flatulence is the scientific name for farting. It's nothing to do with being flat – although you might feel a bit flattened after being given this diagnosis.

TEN THINGS YOU ALWAYS WANTED TO KNOW ABOUT FARTING BUT WERE AFRAID TO ASK

1 Kings and Queens fart. Presidents fart and so do Emperors. Children fart and even teachers are said to do it once in a while. The only difference is how much, how often and how loudly they let it out.

2 The first known account of farting was by ancient Greek playwright Aristophanes (about 448–380 BC) who makes a character in one of his plays say,

"My wind exploded like a thunderclap."

Sounds nasty.

3 Farting is simply your body's way of getting rid of air that you've swallowed by eating too fast, talking while eating, or swallowing bubbly spit. Of course, you can burp some air up. The more you burp, the less you fart. Better not try explaining this important principle at family meal-times.

Or this one…

4 This air gets mixed up with poo in the gut. If there's a lot of air in poo it'll float.

5 Amazingly, a group of fearless scientists analysed the chemical ingredients of a fart. (Did they wear gas masks?) They bravely discovered that a fart is a mixture of five different gases – mainly nitrogen (59 per cent) which is a boring gas that floats about in the air without people taking too much notice of it. Except when someone farts!

6 Well, the smell comes from the chemicals indole and skatole. These are given off when germs get to work on bits of protein from your food.

7 Sometimes a gas called hydrogen sulphide forms in farts. This happens when chemicals from different foods get together in the guts. You'll know all about it because the fart smells like rotten eggs. It's bad news – and not only in the social sense. Hydrogen sulphide is poisonous and it can explode if too much of it mixes with oxygen in the air.

Crisps are full of little air bubbles. Chewing gum makes you swallow air. Like the air in crisps this may re-emerge as farts. Fizzy drinks are full of bubbles.

8 Beans, brussel sprouts, cauliflowers and bran contain a type of carbohydrate that the germs in your gut can change into gas.

Scientists reckon that meat contains many of the chemicals that cause some of the smelliest farts.

9 US astronauts are banned from eating certain foods, especially beans, before a space-flight. Well, how would you fancy being cooped up in a cramped spacecraft on a ten-day space mission with someone who had a bit of a bottom problem?

10 Mind you, flying can make you fart. As a plane flies higher the air pressure around the passengers drops. This makes the air in the guts expand and the result is . . . well, I think you can guess.

When it comes to getting rid of smells there is one invention that has proved more than a flush in the pan.

FLUSHED WITH SUCCESS

1 The world's first flush toilets were invented by people in the Indus Valley of Pakistan over 3,500 years ago. In some towns nearly every house had its very own luxury loo.

CRIKEY! ARE YOU OK IN THERE?

DON'T WORRY, IT'S THE NEW FLUSHING SYSTEM, NOT ME

WHOOSH

2 In the Middle Ages most people had toilets that were nothing more than seats over smelly holes in the ground.

NOW WASH YE hands

3 In 1590, Englishman Sir John Harrington invented a loo that could be flushed with water.
4 But the loo really came into its own after 1778 when inventor Joseph Bramah devised the ball valve which automatically filled the cistern and the "U" bend.

5 Gradually toilets became more and more popular with anyone rich enough to afford them.

But there was a problem.

SOMETHING IN THE AIR

The problem had been festering for some time, growing ever more gross, ever nastier with each passing year. And with each year the truth became ever more unpalatable, ever more horrible. London, one of the greatest cities in the world, stank. It didn't just pong, whiff or smell – it STANK. By the 1850s it reeked of rotting sewage and filth and every kind of loathsome rubbish. And it stank because London's sewerage system had broken down.

The London Times
4th August 1857

A BIG JOB?

Today we bring you an exclusive interview with genuine London "tosher" - Bert Smellie. Bert's unenviable job is to crawl into the sewers in search of valuables accidentally flushed down toilets.

On a good day Bert finds coins, bits of rag and bones. "The work's all right," he says, "it's good money but it's dangerous too!"

"What sort of dangers?" I ask him.

"Them sewers is diabolical," says Bert. "Falling to bits - they can fall on you without warning and you'd be

Bert Smellie

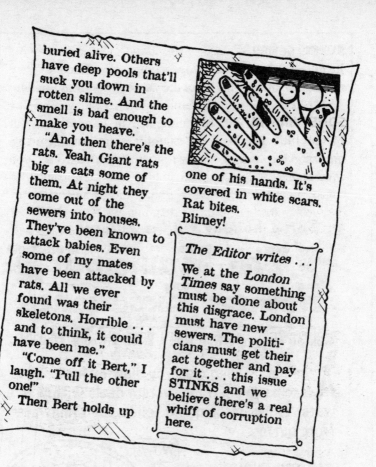

buried alive. Others have deep pools that'll suck you down in rotten slime. And the smell is bad enough to make you heave.

"And then there's the rats. Yeah. Giant rats big as cats some of them. At night they come out of the sewers into houses. They've been known to attack babies. Even some of my mates have been attacked by rats. All we ever found was their skeletons. Horrible . . . and to think, it could have been me."

"Come off it Bert," I laugh. "Pull the other one!"

Then Bert holds up one of his hands. It's covered in white scars. Rat bites. Blimey!

The Editor writes . . .

We at the *London Times* say something must be done about this disgrace. London must have new sewers. The politicians must get their act together and pay for it . . . this issue STINKS and we believe there's a real whiff of corruption here.

Eventually the sewers couldn't take it any more. And so began the Great Stink. It was the most horrible smell anyone could remember. In the hot summer of 1858 the smell of the sewage-clogged River Thames was so foul that people were physically sick. Eventually people kicked up such a stink about it that the politicians were forced to act. The problem was so urgent that the Government agreed to fork out for a brand new sewerage system. At once!

SUPER SEWERS

In all, 209 km of new sewers were constructed. They mainly ran downhill to take the waste away from London. And the system is still operating today. Nowadays complex sewage systems are commonplace in large cities. But in the 19th century some of them were considered so amazing that they became tourist attractions. Can you imagine it?

For a holiday with a difference . . .

The Municipal Sewage Experience

GREAT VALUE - IT WON'T BE A DRAIN ON YOUR POCKET!

A unique thrilling close-up view of how our fascinating sewage system deals with waste water from washing and toilets, and rainwater from gutters.

GASP WITH AMAZEMENT

as the watery mass of sewage is filtered to remove large objects and then left to settle.

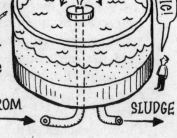

WOW!

FANTASTIC!

WATER FROM DRAINS ➞

➞ SLUDGE

152

BE TOTALLY GOBSMACKED

as watery waste is left in tanks where much of it is eaten by hungry germs. Or we can use the poison chlorine to bump them off!

HOLD YOUR BREATH as the

sludgy solid sewage is left for a few weeks for germs to feast on.

YES, NOTHING IS WASTED

This pongy process gives off smelly gas that can be used to power the sewage works. And it can even be used to light gaslights in the streets. Even the smelly sludge is dried and used as fertilizer.

153

So sewage makes excellent plant food! Ideally suited for growing crops. Crops to make into a school lunch.

A school lunch. But that's where this book started, isn't it?

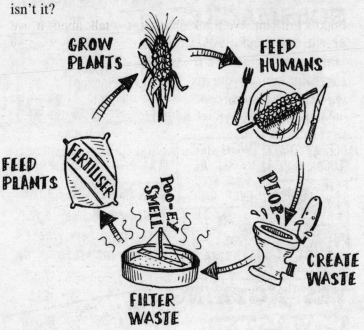

GROW PLANTS

FEED HUMANS

FEED PLANTS

FERTILISER

POO-EY SMELL

PLOP!

CREATE WASTE

FILTER WASTE

SOMETHING TO CHEW OVER (FOOD FOR THOUGHT)

Food's brilliant. We think about it, we talk about it, we even dream about it. And when it's on our plates we play with it before we eat it. But what goes inside our bodies is even more fascinating.

If your digestive system was a machine it would be the most amazing and incredible machine ever invented. Every day it systematically sorts through whatever you choose to feed it with. It sorts out the bits your body can use and chucks out the bits it can't.

All the time you're busy watching TV, sitting in a science lesson or chatting with your friends, your guts are quietly (leaving aside the odd gurgle) getting on with this vital task. They hardly ever protest – OK, so they make you throw up from time to time, but only if they've got a good reason.

So how long has it taken you to read the first bit of this chapter? About one minute? Right, prepare to be amazed… In just one minute:

- Your stomach has churned three times.
- 500,000 new cells have been made for lining your stomach.
- The food in your guts has moved 2.5 cm.

• And your kidneys might have filtered out 1.4 ml of urine that even now could be trickling into your bladder.
• Meanwhile all the glands and organs in your digestive system are happily pumping and squirting away: salivary glands, stomach, liver pancreas. All of them producing their vital juices and enzymes.

And so it carries on 24 hours a day. Even when you're asleep. Even when you're in a science lesson and not thinking about food at all. You've got to admit, it's fascinatingly disgusting.

DISGUSTING DIGESTION QUIZ

Now find out if you're a
Disgusting Digestion expert!

Can you stomach it?

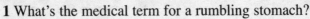

Your digestive system may gurgle like a drain and produce more wind than a Force 9 gale, but it's still a biological miracle. Try this tricky test and see if you know your enzymes from your appendix.

1 What's the medical term for a rumbling stomach?
a) Eructation
b) Borborygmus
c) Regurgitation

2 In which two areas of the body is blood made?
a) Liver
b) Stomach
c) Bone marrow
d) Guts
e) Spleen
f) Pancreas

3 Where would you find the Islets of Langerhans?
a) In the sea.
b) In your kidneys.
c) In the pancreas.

4 What does the appendix do?
a) Breaks down food.
b) Kills germs in the guts.
c) Nothing.

5 How do enzymes work?
a) They stick food molecules together so they can be digested by the guts.
b) They help to split up food molecules until they are small enough to be absorbed by the gut walls.
c) They heat up food molecules to warm up the body and provide energy.

6 How much food does a person eat in their lifetime?
a) 10 tonnes
b) 30 tonnes
c) 100 tonnes

7 How many types of taste can your tongue detect?
a) 3
b) 4
c) 5

8 Lack of vitamin C causes an illness that gives you smelly breath, bleeding eyeballs and swollen gums and can even kill you. What's it called?
a) Scurvy
b) Rickets
c) Green monkey disease

9 What are your molar and premolar teeth used for?
a) Crushing food
b) Tearing food
c) Slicing food

10 What is a pus-filled hole in a tooth called?
a) A scab
b) An abscess
c) A pimple

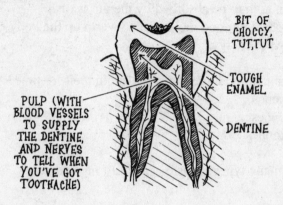

BIT OF CHOCCY, TUT,TUT

TOUGH ENAMEL

DENTINE

PULP (WITH BLOOD VESSELS TO SUPPLY THE DENTINE, AND NERVES TO TELL WHEN YOU'VE GOT TOOTHACHE)

Answers:
1b; 2c and **e;** The bone marrow and the spleen.
3c; 4c That's right. Nothing – not a sausage! **5b;**
6b; 7c; They are sweet, sour, salty, bitter and umami;
8a; 9a; 10b

Busting a gut

Take the strain and try these gut-wrenching, brain-teasing questions – like one of Typhoid Mary's delightful dishes, they'll keep you on the go for ages!

1 What was the name of Versalius's ground-breaking book, published in 1543?
a) *The Fabric of the Human Body*
b) *Guts – The Ultimate Guide*
c) *Versalius's Anatomy*

2 What delicious but deadly dessert did Typhoid Mary make that killed so many people in New York in 1909?
a) Chocolate cake
b) Ice cream
c) Jam roly poly

3 Which ancient Roman wrote over 500 books on medicine?
a) Julius Caesar
b) Claudius Galen
c) Nero

4 How did the scientist Andreas Versalius spend his spare-time?
a) Playing football
b) Dissecting animals
c) Grave-robbing

5 Why did some people in Papua New Guinea eat the brains of their dead relatives?
a) It was considered to be respectful to the dead and a good way to make yourself brainier!
b) They didn't have enough food to eat.
c) They wanted the extra vitamins.

6 In fifth-century India, what did doctors use to hold the gut walls together after an operation to remove a blockage?
a) Thread
b) Ants
c) Sticky tape

7 In ancient China, doctors believed that the appearance of a certain part of your body reflected the health of the rest of your body.
Was it:
a) Your nose
b) Your big toe
c) Your tongue

8 In which part of the world is it considered polite to burp after a meal?
a) England
b) Japan
c) Arabia

9 Which doctor sold poisonous antimony pills in 1733 as a cure for everything?
a) Ned Ford
b) Ned Ward
c) Fred Ward

10 What is the name of the gas that makes farts smell like rotten eggs?
a) Hydrogen sulphide
b) Nitrous oxide
c) Hydrogen peroxide

Answers: 1a; 2b Typhoid germs were transferred from her hands into her handmade ice cream. You wouldn't want her to be cooking your school dinners! **3b; 4c; 5a; 6b;** They used the jaws of ants to bite the sides of the wound together like a stitch. **7c; 8c; 9b; 10a**

Chew it over

Here are some toothy teasers and disgusting digestive queries – you may find some of them a little hard to swallow! What's the missing word or phrase in these foul facts?

1 Every day the tiny Etruscan shrew scoffs up to _____ times its own weight.
a) one
b) five
c) three

2 Several types of _____ can live in people's guts.
a) worm
b) spider
c) snail

3 It _____ to taste your food if you hold your nose when eating.
a) is easier
b) is harder
c) is quicker

4 _____ germs are found in the nostrils and on skin, and can cause diarrhoea, vomiting and cramps in the guts.
a) Staphylococcus
b) Listeria
c) Salmonella

5 The human intestine is _____ long.
a) 9 metres
b) 15 metres
c) 5 metres

6 In the Middle Ages doctors looked at _____ to work out cause of illnesses.
a) spit
b) blood
c) urine

7 Cows have _____ stomachs.
a) two
b) four
c) six

8 A bezoar stone is found in the guts of some animals. It forms from _____.
a) swallowed air.
b) waste food and minerals.
c) blood.

9 If you don't get enough iodine in your diet your _____ gland swells up and forms a horrible lump called a goitre.
a) pineal
b) salivary
c) thyroid

10 Your hypothalamus is a _____ lump on the underside of your brain that signals to your brain when it's time to eat and when to stop.
a) tangerine-sized
b) pea-sized
c) tennis-ball sized

Answers: 1a; 2a This includes roundworms, pin worms and flukes. **3b** It is harder as you can't smell the food – your senses of smell and taste are connected. **4a; 5a; 6c** Some doctors tasted it to test it too! **7b** One stomach stores grass before it's sicked up and the other three store grass as it rots. **8b; 9c; 10b**

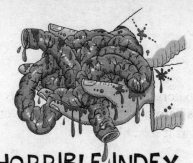

HORRIBLE INDEX

169

170

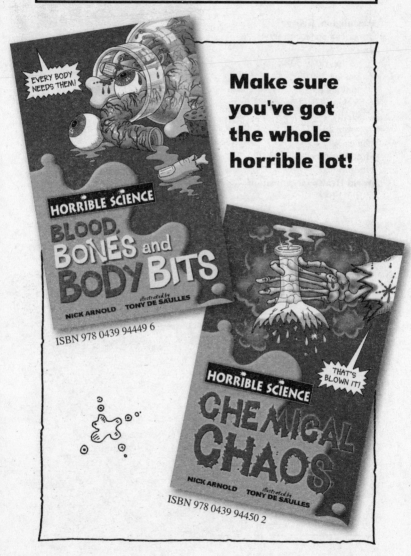

HORRIBLE SCIENCE

NASTY
NATURE

I LOVE
FAST FOOD!

NICK ARNOLD   illustrated by TONY DE SAULLES

ISBN 978 0439 94451 9

IT'S A
GRAVE
SITUATION

HORRIBLE SCIENCE

DEADLY
DISEASES

NICK ARNOLD   illustrated by TONY DE SAULLES

ISBN 978 0439 94445 8

NOT A
PRETTY
SIGHT!

HORRIBLE SCIENCE

UGLY
BUGS

NICK ARNOLD   illustrated by TONY DE SAULLES

ISBN 978 0439 94452 6

HORRIBLE SCIENCE

Science with the squishy bits left in!

Ugly Bugs • Blood, Bones and Body Bits
Nasty Nature • Chemical Chaos • Fatal Forces
Sounds Dreadful • Evolve or Die • Vicious Veg
Disgusting Digestion • Bulging Brains
Frightening Light • Shocking Electricity
Deadly Diseases • Microscopic Monsters
Killer Energy • The Body Owner's Handbook
The Terrible Truth About Time
Space, Stars and Slimy Aliens • Painful Poison
The Fearsome Fight For Flight • Angry Animals
Measly Medicine • Evil Inventions

Specials
Suffering Scientists
Explosive Experiments
The Awfully Big Quiz Book
Really Rotten Experiments

Horrible Science Handbooks
Freaky Food Experiments
Famously Foul Experiments
Beastly Body Experiments

Colour Books
The Stunning Science of Everything
Dangerous Dinosaurs Jigsaw Book